SAS® Technical Report P-221
SAS/ACCESS® Software:
Changes and Enhancements

Release 6.07

SAS Institute Inc.
SAS Campus Drive
Cary, NC 27513

The correct bibliographic citation for this manual is as follows: SAS Institute Inc., SAS' Technical Report P-221, *SAS/ACCESS' Software: Changes and Enhancements, Release 6.07,* Cary, NC: SAS Institute Inc., 1991. 122 pp.

SAS' Technical Report P-221, SAS/ACCESS' Software: Changes and Enhancements, Release 6.07

The SAS' System is an integrated system of software providing complete control over data access, management, analysis, and presentation. Base SAS software is the foundation of the SAS System. Products within the SAS System include SAS/ACCESS; SAS/AF; SAS/ASSIST; SAS/CPE; SAS/DMI; SAS/ETS; SAS/FSP; SAS/GRAPH; SAS/IML; SAS/IMS-DL/I; SAS/OR; SAS/QC; SAS/REPLAY-CICS; SAS/SHARE; SAS/STAT; SAS/CALC; SAS/CONNECT; SAS/DB2; SAS/EIS; SAS/INSIGHT; SAS/LOOKUP; SAS/NVISION; SAS/PH-Clinical; SAS/SQL-DS; and SAS/TOOLKIT" software. Other SAS Institute products are SYSTEM 2000° Data Management Software, with basic SYSTEM 2000, CREATE; Multi-User; QueX; Screen Writer; and CICS interface software; NeoVisuals' software; JMP; JMP IN; JMP SERVE; and JMP Ahead" software; SAS/RTERM' software; and the SAS/C' Compiler and the SAS/CX' Compiler. MultiVendor Architecture" and MVA" are trademarks of SAS Institute Inc. *SAS Communications; SAS Training; SAS Views;* the SASware Ballot; and *Observations"* are published by SAS Institute Inc. All trademarks above are registered trademarks or trademarks of SAS Institute Inc. in the USA and other countries. ® indicates USA registration.

The Institute is a private company devoted to the support and further development of its software and related services.

DB2' and SQL/DS" are registered trademarks or trademarks of International Business Machines Corporation.

Other brand and product names are registered trademarks or trademarks of their respective companies.

Doc S19, Ver 112.0, 110891

Contents

Reference Aids

Figures

Tables

Using This Book

Purpose

This document provides a summary of the Release 6.07 changes and enhancements to SAS/ACCESS software. Use this technical report as an addendum to your copy of the appropriate SAS/ACCESS software documentation.

Audience

This report is intended for applications programmers and users who know how to use their operating system but who may not be familiar with the SAS System or any of the database management systems with which SAS/ACCESS software interfaces. This report is also intended for users of Release 6.06 of SAS/ACCESS software who plan to upgrade their systems to Release 6.07. Database Administrators (DBAs) may also want to read this report to understand how Release 6.07 of SAS/ACCESS software works and how they should administer it.

Prerequisites

The following table summarizes the concepts you need to understand in order to use this book:

You need to know	Refer to
how your operating system works with Version 6 of the SAS System	the Version 6 SAS companion for your operating system
names of the database management system databases or tables you want to use	instructions provided by your DBA
how to create Version 6 access descriptors and view descriptors	the Version 6 SAS/ACCESS interface book for your DBMS
how to invoke the SAS System at your site	the instructions provided by the SAS Software Consultant at your site
how to reference SAS files	*SAS Language: Reference, Version 6, First Edition.*

If you would like more details on either the SAS System or the SAS/ACCESS interface to your database management system, refer to the documents listed in "Additional Documentation" later in this chapter.

Using this report also involves these prerequisites:

☐ base SAS software, Release 6.07 or later

☐ SAS/ACCESS interface to the specific database management systems

☐ the database management system software required for your SAS/ACCESS interface product.

How to Use This Book

This section gives an overview of this book's organization and content.

Organization

SAS Technical Report P-221, *SAS/ACCESS Software: Changes and Enhancements, Release 6.07*, contains six chapters as detailed in the following list.

Chapter 1, "SAS/ACCESS Interfaces to DB2, ORACLE, Rdb/VMS, and SQL/DS Data Management Software"
  describes the Release 6.07 changes and enhancements to the SAS/ACCESS interfaces to the DB2, ORACLE, Rdb/VMS, and SQL/DS relational database management systems.

Chapter 2, "SAS/ACCESS Interface to SYSTEM 2000 Data Management Software,"
  describes the Release 6.07 changes and enhancements to the SAS/ACCESS interface to SYSTEM 2000 data management software.

Chapter 3, "SAS/ACCESS Interface to ADABAS Data Management Software,"
  describes the changes and enhancements to the SAS/ACCESS interface to the ADABAS data management software.

Chapter 4, "SAS/ACCESS Interface to CA-DATACOM/DB Data Management Software,"
  describes the Release 6.07 changes and enhancements to the SAS/ACCESS interface to the CA-DATACOM/DB data management software.

Chapter 5, "The SQL Procedure,"
  describes the Release 6.07 enhancements to the SQL procedure that interact with SAS/ACCESS software.

Chapter 6, "Version 5 Database Interfaces,"
  summarizes the upward compatibility changes to SAS/DB2 and SAS/SQL-DS software in Version 5 of the SAS System.

Each chapter first presents a synopsis of the changes and enhancements documented in that chapter. Then more detailed information is provided.
  You should read the chapter that documents your data management system. Depending upon your information goals, you should read the other chapters as needed.

Reference Aids

The index, located at the end of this guide, provides a cross-reference of the pages where specific topics and terms are discussed in this book.

Conventions

This section covers the conventions this book uses, including typographical conventions and syntax conventions.

Typographical Conventions

In this book, you will see several type styles used. Style conventions are summarized here:

roman | is the basic type style used for most text.

UPPERCASE ROMAN | is used for references in the text to keywords of the SAS language, filenames, variable names, and commands.

italic | is used to emphasize important information.

`monospace` | is used to show examples of SAS code. In most cases, this book uses lowercase for SAS code, with the exception of some title characters. You can enter your own SAS code in lowercase, uppercase, or a mixture of the two. The SAS System always changes your variable names to uppercase, but character variable values remain in lowercase if you have entered them that way. Enter any titles and footnotes exactly as you want them to appear on your output.
  Monospace is also used for character variable values that appear in text.

Syntax Conventions

The following conventions are used to present the syntax of SAS statements and commands:

bold | indicates primary parts of the SAS language: statement, function, and procedure names. For these terms, you must use the exact spelling shown.

UPPERCASE ROMAN | indicates arguments whose values have the exact spelling shown. The argument may or may not be optional, depending on whether it is enclosed in angle brackets (<>). Note that you do not have to use uppercase when you type these arguments.

italic	indicates items in statement syntax (arguments) for which you supply a value.
<arguments in angle brackets>	are optional. Multiple arguments within one set of brackets means that if you use one argument, you must use all the arguments.
arguments not in angle brackets	are required.
. . . (ellipsis)	indicates that multiple sets of arguments can be specified. If the ellipsis and the final set of arguments are enclosed in angle brackets, they are optional.
| (vertical bar)	means to choose one item from a group of the items separated by the bars.

The following example (an excerpt from the ACCESS procedure syntax) illustrates these syntax conventions:

PROC ACCESS ACCDESC=<*libref.*>*access-descriptor* FUNCTION=C
      DBMS=*database-product*;
  DROP <*item-name-n* \| *index-number-n*> . . . ;
  FORMAT <*item-name-n* \| *index-number-n*> <=>
     format . . . ;
  LIST <ALL \| VIEW \| *index-number-n* \| *item-name-n*>
    <*blanks* \| DB \| DESC>;
  RENAME <*item-name-n* \| *index-name-n*> <=>
    SAS-name . . . ;
  RESET <ALL \| <*item-name-n* \| *index-number-n*>> . . . ;
  SELECT <ALL \| <*item-name-n* \| *index-number-n*>> . . . ;

PROC ACCESS
  is a primary part of the language so it appears in boldface type. PROC ACCESS is the procedure's name.

DBMS=*database product*
  is required because it is not enclosed in angle brackets. The uppercase roman type indicates that the DBMS value must be spelled as shown in the syntax.

<*item-name-n* \| *index-number-n*> . . . ;
  is optional because it is enclosed in angle brackets. The vertical bar indicates that only one of these values can be specified. The ellipsis indicates that you can specify more than one item name or index number.

Conventions for Examples and Output

The examples in the chapters show you how to combine statements and options to achieve the results you want. You can run any of the examples in this book as you read the chapters. Most examples use permanent SAS data sets because several examples in a chapter or part may use the same data set.

Each page of output produced by a procedure is enclosed in a box and given a title. Most of the programs in this book were run using the following SAS system options:

PAGESIZE=60   sets the length of the page to 60 lines.

LINESIZE=80   sets the length of the text line to 80 characters.

NODATE   indicates you do not want the date and time to appear in your output.

Conventions for Issuing SAS System Commands

With Version 6 of the SAS System, there are three methods of issuing SAS System commands: the command line, function keys, and the PMENU facility. As you use the interface, you can choose any of the three methods, but this book illustrates only the command-line method.

The function keys are predefined by the SAS System. To determine or change their settings, use the KEYS window.

The PMENU facility is new in Version 6 of the SAS System. It enables you to work within the windows using menu selections. To turn on the menus, simply enter PMENU on the command line. Then use the cursor and tab keys, or a mouse if you have one, to move through the menus. You can do most things with the PMENU facility that you can do with command-line commands, with the advantage that you do not have to remember the command names. For more information on the PMENU facility, see Chapter 7, "SAS Display Manager System," in *SAS Language: Reference, Version 6, First Edition*.

Running the SAS System

The following table summarizes the different methods of running the SAS System:

Method of Operation	What you can do
Display manager mode	Create descriptors using windows
	Create descriptors using procedure statements
Interactive line mode	Create descriptors using procedure statements
	Create descriptors using windows (if your terminal supports it)
Noninteractive mode	Create descriptors using procedure statements
Batch mode	Create descriptors using procedure statements

Refer to Chapter 1, "Essential Concepts," in *SAS Language: Reference, Version 6, First Edition*, for more information on the different methods of running the SAS System.

(NODATE continued)

Additional Documentation

The following sections list documentation that may be helpful when you are using the SAS System or SAS/ACCESS software.

SAS Documentation

There are many SAS System publications available. To receive a free *Publications Catalog*, write to the following address or call Book Sales at the following number:

> SAS Institute Inc.
> Book Sales Department
> SAS Campus Drive
> Cary, NC 27513
> (919) 677-8000

The books listed here will help you find answers to questions you may have about the SAS System in general or specific aspects of the SAS System, such as SAS/FSP software.

□ *SAS Language and Procedures: Introduction, Version 6, First Edition* (order #A56074) gets you started if you are unfamiliar with the SAS System or any programming language.

□ *SAS Language and Procedures: Usage, Version 6, First Edition* (order #A56075) is a user's guide to the SAS System. It shows you how to use base SAS software for data analysis, report writing, and data manipulation. It also includes information on processing methods.

□ *SAS Language: Reference, Version 6, First Edition* (order #A56076) provides detailed information on base SAS software, the SAS programming language, and the types of applications the SAS System can perform. Chapter 6, "SAS Files," explains how the implementation of SAS data sets has changed in Version 6 of the SAS System.

□ *SAS Procedures Guide, Version 6, Third Edition* (order #A56080) provides detailed information about the procedures available in the base SAS software.

□ *SAS/FSP Software: Usage and Reference, Version 6, First Edition* (order #A56001) shows you how to use the FSBROWSE, FSEDIT, and FSVIEW procedures.

□ *SAS Companion for the MVS Environment, Version 6, First Edition* (order #A56101) describes how to use the SAS System with the host MVS operating system.

□ *SAS Guide to the SQL Procedure: Usage and Reference, Version 6, First Edition* (order #A56070) shows you how to use the SQL procedure, which implements the Structured Query Language on Version 6 of the SAS System. You can use the SQL procedure to join and manipulate the data accessed by SAS/ACCESS views and other SAS data sets.

❏ The following interface guides explain how to use the SAS/ACCESS software with other software vendors' products. They explain how to create SAS/ACCESS descriptor files and provide more information on using them in SAS programs. For a complete list of SAS/ACCESS interface guides, consult the *Publications Catalog*.

   ❏ *SAS/ACCESS Interface to ADABAS: Usage and Reference, Version 6, First Edition* (order #A56065)

   ❏ *SAS/ACCESS Interface to CA-DATACOM/DB: Usage and Reference, Version 6, First Edition* (order #A56066)

   ❏ *SAS/ACCESS Interface to DB2: Usage and Reference, Version 6, First Edition* (order #A56060)

   ❏ *SAS/ACCESS Interface to IMS-DL/I: Usage and Reference, Version 6, First Edition* (order #A56069)

   ❏ *SAS/ACCESS Interface to INGRES: Usage and Reference, Version 6, First Edition* (order #A56072)

   ❏ *SAS/ACCESS Interface to ORACLE: Usage and Reference, Version 6, First Edition* (order #A56061)

   ❏ *SAS/ACCESS Interface to Prime INFORMATION: Usage and Reference, Version 6, First Edition* (order #A56067)

   ❏ *SAS/ACCESS Interface to Rdb/VMS: Usage and Reference, Version 6, First Edition* (order #A56062)

   ❏ *SAS/ACCESS Interface to SQL/DS: Usage and Reference, Version 6, First Edition* (order #A56063)

   ❏ *SAS/ACCESS Interface to SYSTEM 2000 Data Management Software: Usage and Reference, Version 6, First Edition* (order #A56064)

❏ SAS Technical Report P-216, *SAS/AF Software, SAS/FSP Software, and SAS Screen Control Language: Changes and Enhancements, Release 6.07* (order #A59133) describes changes and enhancements to SAS/AF software, SAS/FSP software, and SCL.

❏ SAS Technical Report P-222, *Changes and Enhancements to Base SAS Software, Release 6.07* (order #A59139) describes Release 6.07 changes and enhancements to the base SAS System.

❏ SAS Technical Report P-223, *SAS/CONNECT Software: Changes and Enhancements for the CMS, MVS, and VMS Environments, Release 6.07* (order #A59140) describes Release 6.07 changes and enhancements to SAS/CONNECT software.

Other Vendor Documentation

To get a list of books about your DBMS, see "Using This Book" in the Version 6 SAS/ACCESS book for your product.

Changes and Enhancements

Introduction

This section summarizes the changes and enhancements to SAS/ACCESS software for Release 6.07 since Release 6.06. It is intended for users who have previous experience with SAS/ACCESS software. Changes and enhancements are presented in a broad outline. For more detail, refer to the appropriate chapter in this technical report.

Overview of Changes and Enhancements

Release 6.07 offers the following changes and enhancements to the SAS/ACCESS interfaces to DB2, ORACLE, Rdb/VMS, SQL/DS, and SYSTEM 2000 Database Management Software:

☐ enhancements that enable you to create access and view descriptors in interactive line, noninteractive, and batch modes. You can still run the ACCESS procedure in display manager mode. This flexibility enables you to choose a method for creating access and view descriptors based on your environment and personal preferences.

☐ enhancements to PROC ACCESS syntax, including new options and statements.

☐ enhancements to PROC DBLOAD syntax for ORACLE to support ORACLE's SQL*NET drivers.

Release 6.07 offers the following changes and enhancements to the SAS/ACCESS interfaces to ADABAS and CA-DATACOM/DB:

☐ changes to the way SAS system options are specified

☐ changes to the WHERE clause.

Release 6.07 offers the following general changes and enhancements to SAS/ACCESS software:

☐ enhancements that provide password capability. You can now assign passwords to any kind of data set, including descriptors.

☐ modifications to the SQL procedure enabling it to support rollbacks of group updates for databases supporting member- or record-level locking.

☐ enhancements enabling you to use the SQL Pass-Through facility to pass SQL statements directly to a database management system for processing.

This technical report documents changes and enhancements to Release 6.07 of the SAS System, not to SAS/ACCESS software. These changes and enhancements include upward compatibility changes to SAS/DB2 and SAS/SQL-DS software.

Chapter **1** SAS/ACCESS® Interfaces to DB2, ORACLE, Rdb/VMS, and SQL/DS Data Management Software

Introduction

This chapter describes the Release 6.07 changes and enhancements in the SAS/ACCESS interfaces to DB2, ORACLE, Rdb/VMS, and SQL/DS. These interfaces are all for relational database management systems.

With Release 6.07 of the SAS System, you can run the ACCESS procedure in interactive line, noninteractive, and batch modes, as well as in display manager mode (as described in your Release 6.06 SAS/ACCESS documentation). This flexibility enables you to choose a method for creating access descriptors and view descriptors based on your environment and personal preferences.

Also, Release 6.07 provides a SAS System password capability. You can assign passwords to access descriptors and to any kind of SAS data set. This chapter briefly describes how to assign passwords to access and view descriptors.

This chapter also includes a section listing the changes and enhancements to the DBLOAD procedure in Release 6.07 of the SAS System.

ACCESS Procedure

The following section describes changes to the ACCESS procedure for Release 6.07 of the SAS System.

Syntax

This section describes the PROC ACCESS statement options and procedure statements added in Release 6.07 of the SAS System. These options enable you to run the ACCESS procedure in display manager mode or you can use the options and statements to run PROC ACCESS steps in interactive line, noninteractive, or batch mode. See "Running the SAS System" in "Using This Book" for more information on these SAS methods of operation. The syntax for creating access and view descriptors in display manager mode has not changed.

The ACCESS procedure's basic syntax for creating access descriptors and view descriptors is the same for DB2, ORACLE, Rdb/VMS, and SQL/DS. The only differences lie in the statements you use to identify the database, which are described later in this chapter. Here is the basic syntax:

PROC ACCESS
    ACCDESC=*libref.access-descriptor*
    ALIB=*libref*
    DBMS=*database-management-system*
    FUNCTION=C | U | ED
    OUT=*libref.member*
    VIEWDESC=*libref.view-descriptor*;
  CREATE *libref.member-name.type*;
  database-identification-statements;
  ASSIGN<=>YES | NO;
  DROP *column-identifier-1* <. . . *column-identifier-n*>;
  FORMAT *column-identifier-1*<=>*SAS-format-name-1*
    <. . . *column-identifier-n*<=>*SAS-format-name-n*>;
  LIST <ALL | VIEW | *list-selection*>;
  QUIT;
  RENAME *column-identifier-1*<=>*SAS-variable-name-1*
    <. . . *column-identifier-n*<=>*SAS-variable-name-n*>;
  RESET ALL | *column-identifier-1* <. . . *column-identifier-n*>;
  SELECT ALL | *column-identifier-1* <. . . *column-identifier-n*>;
  SUBSET *selection-criteria*;
  UNIQUE<=>YES | NO;

For interactive line mode, enter these statements at the ? prompt. For noninteractive and batch jobs, surround your SAS statements with any appropriate operating system-specific statements and submit the job for processing.

PROC ACCESS Statement Options

The following options can be used with the PROC ACCESS statement. The options you use depend on your goal (creating an access descriptor, editing a view descriptor, and so on) and on the method of operation you choose. For easier reference, all the PROC ACCESS options are described in this section, including those that have not changed in Release 6.07.

Most of the options can only be used with a particular method of operation, which is highlighted in boldface. This section distinguishes between **display manager mode** and the **other modes,** (that is, interactive line, noninteractive, or batch). See "Running the SAS System" in "Using This Book" for more information on these SAS methods of operation.

ACCDESC=*libref.access-descriptor*   **(all modes)**
ACCESS=
AD=
    identifies an access descriptor.

    Other modes: You use this option to create view descriptors from an existing access descriptor.

    If the access descriptor has been assigned a SAS password, you may need to specify the password in the ACCDESC= option in order to create a view descriptor based on the access descriptor. Whether you specify the password depends on the level of protection that was assigned to the access descriptor. For example, the following access descriptor, SASUSER.SALARIES, has a password (MONEY) assigned to it with the ALTER level of protection. Therefore, the password must be specified using the ALTER= SAS data option before you are allowed to create view descriptors based on SASUSER.SALARIES.

```
proc access dbms=db2 accdesc=sasuser.salaries(alter=money);
```

See "Specifying SAS System Passwords for SAS/ACCESS Descriptors" later in this chapter for more information on assigning and using passwords.

    If you create the access descriptor and the view descriptor in the same execution of PROC ACCESS, omit the ACCDESC= option because you specify the access descriptor's name in the CREATE statement.

    Display manager mode: You can use the ACCDESC= option (in combination with the FUNCTION= option) to create an access descriptor and bypass the ACCESS window. See the Release 6.06 documentation for your SAS/ACCESS interface for more information and examples.

    AD= and ACCESS= are aliases for this option.

ALIB=*libref*   **(display manager mode only)**
    specifies the SAS data library that contains the access descriptor for the view descriptor you want to edit. You use the ALIB= option in conjunction with the VIEWDESC= option.

    If you omit this option, the SAS System searches all SAS data libraries allocated to your session until it finds an access descriptor with the correct name. Using the ALIB= option may save you time if you have several SAS data libraries allocated to your SAS session. The ALIB= option also prevents you from using the wrong access descriptor if you have two access descriptors with the same name but in different libraries.

4 Syntax □ Chapter 1

DBMS=*database-management-system*   **(other modes only)**

identifies the DBMS you want to access. The values for this option are DB2, ORACLE, RDB, and SQLDS, depending on your interface. This option is required when creating a descriptor but not when extracting DBMS data. The DBMS= option must immediately follow PROC ACCESS in the PROC statement.

FUNCTION=C | U | ED   **(display manager mode only)**
FUNC=

specifies whether you want to create a new access descriptor or update an existing access descriptor. You specify the FUNCTION= option after the ACCDESC= option.

You specify the C value to create an access descriptor and the U or ED value to update an existing access descriptor. You can edit an access descriptor only using the windows.

In interactive line, noninteractive, and batch modes, the CREATE statement supercedes the FUNCTION=C option. If you specify FUNCTION=C, it is ignored in these modes.

OUT=*libref.member*   **(other modes only)**

identifies the SAS data file that stores extracted DBMS data. You can only use this option after the VIEWDESC= option.

VIEWDESC=*libref.view-descriptor*   **(all modes)**
VIEW=
VD=

identifies a view descriptor.

Display manager mode: You use this option to specify the view descriptor to be edited. You can edit a view descriptor only in this mode.

Other modes: You use the VIEWDESC= option to extract DBMS data and to place them in a SAS data file. When extracting DBMS data, you must specify the OUT= option after the VIEWDESC= option.

See "Examples" later in this chapter for examples of using options in procedure statements.

Procedure Statements

The procedure statements for PROC ACCESS enable you to create access and view descriptors in interactive line mode, noninteractive mode, and batch mode. (See "Running the SAS System" in "Using this Book" for more information on these SAS methods of operation.) The statements you use depend on which DBMS you are using and your purpose, such as creating only an access descriptor, creating only a view descriptor, or creating both types of descriptors.

Portable statements

The following procedure statements are available with PROC ACCESS for the DB2, SQL/DS, ORACLE, and Rdb/VMS interfaces.

CREATE *libref.member-name.type*;

identifies an access descriptor or view descriptor you want to create. The CREATE statement is required.

To create the descriptor, use a three-level name. The first level is the libref of the SAS data library where you want the descriptor stored. You can store the descriptor in a temporary (WORK) or permanent SAS data library. The second level is the access descriptor's name (that is, the member name). The third level is the type of SAS file: ACCESS for access descriptors and VIEW for view descriptors.

When you submit a CREATE statement for processing, the SAS/ACCESS interface checks the statement for errors and, if it doesn't find any errors, writes the previous descriptor if one was specified. If the SAS/ACCESS interface does find errors, error messages are written to the SAS log and processing is terminated. After you correct the error, resubmit the statements for processing.

Creating access descriptors

To create an access descriptor, you must specify a CREATE statement naming the access descriptor. It is specified before any of the database-description or editing statements, such as the RENAME and FORMAT statements. For example, you could specify the following:

```
proc access dbms=DBMS-name;
   create mylib.customer.access;
      database-identification statement(s);
      optional editing statement(s);
run;
```

You can create one or more view descriptors based on this access descriptor within the same execution of the procedure, as described later in this section. See also "Examples" later in this chapter for more DBMS-specific examples.

Creating view descriptors

You also use the CREATE statement to create a view descriptor. You can create a view descriptor in the same execution or in a separate execution of the ACCESS procedure.

To create a view descriptor in the same execution of PROC ACCESS, add the CREATE statement after the procedure statements that create the access descriptor on which this view descriptor is based. For example, you could specify the following:

```
proc access dbms=DBMS-name;
   create mylib.customer.access;
      database-identification statement(s);
      optional editing statement(s);

   create vlib.phonenum.view;
      select column-list;
      optional editing statement(s);
run;
```

If you create a view based on an existing access descriptor (that is, one created in a previous execution of the ACCESS procedure), specify the access descriptor's name in the ACCDESC= option in the PROC ACCESS statement and follow it with a CREATE statement. Place any editing and view

(CREATE libref.member-name.type; continued)

descriptor-specific statements, such as SELECT and SUBSET, after the view descriptor's CREATE statement. For example, you could specify the following:

```
proc access dbms=DBMS-name accdesc=mylib.customer;
    create vlib.bigcust.view;
        select column-list;
        optional editing statement(s);
        subset where-expression;
    create vlib.texcust.view;
        select column-list;
        optional editing statement(s);
run;
```

When you specify the ACCDESC= option in the PROC ACCESS statement, you can use CREATE statements only to create view descriptors. You can issue multiple CREATE statements to create views based on the specified access descriptor. See "Examples" later in this chapter for DBMS-specific examples.

The database-identification statements are not required if you are creating view descriptors because the database information is stored with the access descriptor.

database-identification-statements;

identify the database and table on which you want to create an access descriptor. These statements are database-specific and are described later in this chapter, in sections such as "DB2 Statements" and "ORACLE Statements." When creating an access descriptor, the database-identification statements must follow the CREATE statement.

ASSIGN | AN<=>YES | NO | Y | N;

generates SAS variable names based on the first eight, non-blank characters of the database column names. It also generates SAS variable formats based on the database columns' data types. The ASSIGN statement is specified only when creating an access descriptor. This statement is optional.

The default value NO (or N) permits you to modify SAS variable names and formats when you create the access descriptor and when you create view descriptors based on this access descriptor. You use the RENAME statement to change the SAS variable names during a descriptor's creation.

Specifying a YES (or Y) value for this statement also generates SAS variable names, but these names can only be changed in the access descriptor. The SAS names and formats saved in the access descriptor are always used in view descriptors created from this access descriptor. This statement prevents you from changing SAS variable names and formats when you create a view descriptor.

If you specify a YES value for this statement, the SAS System automatically resolves any duplicate variable names. However, with a YES value, you cannot specify the RENAME, FORMAT, and UNIQUE statements when creating view descriptors based on this access descriptor.

When the interface encounters the next CREATE statement to create an access descriptor, the ASSIGN statement is reset to the default NO value.

AN is the alias for the ASSIGN statement.

DROP *column-identifier-1* <. . . *column-identifier-n*>;

drops the specified column from the access descriptor so that the column is no longer available for selection when creating a view descriptor. The specified column in the database table remains unaffected by this statement. The DROP statement is specified only when creating an access descriptor. This statement is optional.

The *column-identifier* argument can be either the column name or the positional equivalent from the LIST statement, which is the number that represents the column's place in the access descriptor. For example, if you want to drop the third and fifth columns, issue the following statement:

```
drop 3 5;
```

If the column name contains blanks or special characters, enclose the name in quotes. You can drop as many columns as you want in one DROP statement.

If you want to display a column that was previously marked as non-display with the DROP statement, specify that column name in the RESET statement. However, doing so also resets all the column's attributes (such as the SAS variable name and format) to their default values.

FORMAT *column-identifier-1*<=>*SAS-format-name-1*
  <. . . *column-identifier-n*<=>*SAS-format-name-n*>;

changes a SAS variable format from its default format; the default SAS variable format is based on the database column's data type. The FORMAT statement can be used when creating an access descriptor or a view descriptor. This statement is optional.

The *column-identifier* argument can be either the column name or the positional equivalent from the LIST statement, which is the number that represents the column's place in the access descriptor. For example, if you want to associate the DATE9. format with the following columns in the access descriptor, issue the following statement:

```
format 2=date9.  birthdate date9.;
```

Notice that the *column-identifier* is specified on the left and the SAS format on the right of the expression. The equal sign (=) is optional. If the column name contains blanks or special characters, enclose the name in quotes. You can enter formats for as many columns as you want using one FORMAT statement.

You can only use the FORMAT statement with a view descriptor if the ASSIGN statement used when creating the access descriptor was specified with the NO value. When used for a view descriptor, the FORMAT statement automatically selects the reformatted column if it has not been selected previously. That is, if you change the format of the variable associated with a column, you do not have to issue a SELECT statement for that column.

Note: When using the FORMAT statement with access descriptors, the FORMAT statement also reselects columns that were previously dropped with the DROP statement.

FMT is the alias for the FORMAT statement.

LIST <ALL | VIEW | *column-identifier*>;

lists all or selected columns in the descriptor and information about the columns. The LIST statement can be used when creating an access descriptor

(LIST   continued)

or a view descriptor. In noninteractive and batch modes, the LIST information
is written to your SAS log. This statement is optional.

The LIST statement can take one or more of the following arguments:

ALL
    lists all the database columns in the table, the positional
equivalents, the SAS variable names, and SAS variable
formats that are available for the access descriptor. If a
column has been dropped when creating an access
descriptor, `*NON-DISPLAY*` is shown next to the
column's description. When creating a view descriptor,
columns that are selected for the view are shown with
`*SELECTED*` next to the column's description.

    If you do not specify an argument, the default is
ALL.

VIEW
    lists all the database columns in the access descriptor
that are selected for the view descriptor, including their
positional equivalents, the SAS names and formats, and
any subsetting clauses. Any columns dropped in the
access descriptor will not be displayed. The VIEW
argument is only valid when creating a view descriptor.

column-identifier
    lists the database column name, the positional
equivalent, the SAS variable name and format, and
whether the column has been selected. If the column
name contains blanks or special characters, enclose the
name in quotes.

    The *column-identifier* argument can be either the
column name or the positional equivalent, which is the
number that represents the column's place in the
descriptor. For example, if you want to list information
about the fifth column in the descriptor, issue the
following statement:

```
list 5;
```

You can use one or more of these options in a LIST statement, in any
order. Here is an example:

```
list all view;
```

The LIST statement lists all the columns in the descriptor and then repeats the
information by just listing the columns selected for the view descriptor.

QUIT | EXIT;
    terminates the ACCESS procedure without any further descriptor creation.
The QUIT statement can be used when creating a descriptor. This statement is
optional. EXIT is the alias for the QUIT statement.

RENAME *column-identifier-1< = >SAS-variable-name-1*
  <. . . column-identifier-n< = >SAS-variable-name-n;
  enters or modifies the SAS variable name associated with a database column.
  The RENAME statement can be used when creating an access descriptor or a
  view descriptor. This statement is optional.
  Two factors affect the use of the RENAME statement: whether you specify
  the ASSIGN statement when creating an access descriptor and the kind of
  descriptor you are creating:

  □ If you omit the ASSIGN statement or specify it with a NO value, the
    renamed SAS variable names you specify in the access descriptor are
    retained throughout an ACCESS procedure execution. If you rename the
    CUSTOMER column to CUSTNUM when creating an access descriptor,
    that column continues to be named CUSTNUM when you select it in a
    view descriptor based on the access descriptor unless a RESET statement
    or another RENAME statement is specified.
      When creating a view descriptor based on this access descriptor, you
    can specify the RESET statement or another RENAME statement to
    rename the variable again, but the new name applies only in that view.
    When creating other view descriptors, the SAS variable names and
    formats will be derived from the access descriptor.

  □ If you specify the YES value in the ASSIGN statement, you can only use
    the RENAME statement to change SAS variable names while creating an
    access descriptor. As described earlier in the ASSIGN statement, SAS
    variable names and formats saved in the access descriptor are always used
    when creating view descriptors based on it.

  The *column-identifier* argument can be either the column name or the
  positional equivalent from the LIST statement, which is the number that
  represents the column's place in the descriptor. For example, if you want to
  rename the SAS variable names associated with the first and fifth columns in
  a descriptor, issue the following statement:

```
rename 1 custnum telephone=phone;
```

  Notice that the *column-identifier* is specified on the left side and the SAS
  variable name on the right side of the expression. The equal sign (=) is
  optional. If the column name contains blanks or special characters, enclose the
  name in quotes. You can rename as many columns as you want using one
  RENAME statement.
  When creating a view descriptor, the RENAME statement automatically
  selects the renamed column for the view. That is, if you rename the SAS
  variable associated with a database column, you do not have to issue a
  SELECT statement for that column.

RESET ALL | *column-identifier-1 <. . . column-identifier-n>;*
  resets all or the specified columns to their default values. The RESET
  statement can be used when creating an access descriptor or a view
  descriptor; however, it has different effects on these descriptors, as described
  here. The RESET statement is optional.

(RESET ALL continued)

Access descriptors
When creating an access descriptor, the default setting for a SAS variable name is a blank, unless you enter SAS variable names using the RENAME statement or include the ASSIGN=YES statement. If you entered or modified any SAS variable name, the name is reset to the default name generated by the ACCESS procedure (that is, blank or the first eight characters of the database column name).

The current SAS format is reset to the default SAS format, which was determined from the column's data type. Any columns that have been dropped using the DROP statement are now available and can be selected in view descriptors based on this access descriptor.

View descriptors
When creating a view descriptor, the RESET statement clears any columns included in the SELECT statement (that is, it unselects the columns).

When creating the view descriptor, if you reset a SAS variable and then select it again later within the same procedure execution, the SAS variable names and formats are reset to the default values generated from the column names and data types. This applies only if you have omitted the ASSIGN statement or specified the NO value in it when you created the access descriptor on which the view descriptor is based. If you specified the ASSIGN=YES statement when you created the access descriptor, the view descriptor's SAS variable names and formats are unaffected by the RESET statement.

The RESET statement can take one or more of the following arguments:

ALL
: resets all the database columns defined in the access descriptor to their default name and format settings. When creating a view descriptor, the ALL argument resets all the columns that have been selected, so that no columns are selected for the view; you can then use the SELECT statement to select new columns. See the SELECT statement later in this chapter for more information.

column-identifier
: can be either the column name or the positional equivalent from the LIST statement, which is the number that represents the column's place in the access descriptor. For example, if you want to reset the SAS variable name and format associated with the third column, issue the following statement:

```
reset 3;
```

If the column name contains blanks or special characters, enclose the name in quotes. You can reset as many columns as you want using one RESET statement or the ALL option to reset all the columns.

When creating an access descriptor, the
column-identifier is reset to its default name and format
settings. When creating a view descriptor, the specified
column is no longer selected for the view.

SELECT ALL | *column-identifier-1* <. . . *column-identifier-n*>;
  selects the database columns in the access descriptor to be included in the
  view descriptor. This is a required statement and is used only when defining
  view descriptors.
    The SELECT statement can take one or more of the following arguments:

ALL   includes in the view descriptor all the columns defined
                       in the access descriptor that were not dropped.

column-identifier   can be either the column name or the positional
                       equivalent from the LIST statement, which is the
                       number that represents the column's place in the access
                       descriptor on which the view is based. For example, if
                       you want to select the first three columns, issue the
                       following statement:

                           select 1 2 3;

                       If the column name contains blanks or special
                       characters, enclose the name in quotes. You can select
                       as many columns as you want using one SELECT
                       statement.

    SELECT statements are cumulative within the same view creation. That is,
if you submit the following two SELECT statements, columns 1, 5, and 6 are
selected (not just columns 5 and 6):

    select 1;
    select 5 6;

    To clear all your current selections when creating a view descriptor, you
can use the **RESET ALL** statement; you can then use another SELECT
statement to select new columns.

SUBSET *selection-criteria*;
  specifies the selection criteria when creating a view descriptor. The SUBSET
  statement is optional, but omitting it causes the view to retrieve all the data
  (that is, rows) in the database table.
    The *selection-criteria* argument can be one or more of the following SQL
  statements accepted by your DBMS: WHERE, ORDER BY, HAVING, or
  GROUP BY. You use the DBMS column names, not the SAS variable names,
  in your selection criteria. For example, for a view descriptor that retrieves
  rows in an ORACLE table, you could issue the following SUBSET statement:

    subset where salary>60000.00;

If you have multiple selection criteria, enter them all in one SUBSET
statement, as in the following example:

(SUBSET selection-criteria; continued)

```
subset where salary>60000.00 and sex='F'
   order by dept;
```

For more information on what SQL statements you can use with the SAS/ACCESS interface to your DBMS, refer to your Release 6.06 SAS/ACCESS documentation.

To clear the selection criteria, issue a SUBSET statement without an argument, as follows:

```
subset;
```

UNIQUE<=>YES | NO | Y | N;
UN<=>YES | NO | Y | N;
  specifies whether the SAS/ACCESS interface should generate unique SAS variable names for database columns for which SAS variable names have not been entered. The UNIQUE statement is optional and is used only when creating view descriptors.

  Use of the UNIQUE statement is affected by whether you specified the ASSIGN statement when creating the access descriptor on which this view is based.

  □ If you specified the ASSIGN statement with a YES value, you cannot specify the UNIQUE statement when creating a view. The YES value causes the SAS System to generate unique names, so the UNIQUE statement is not necessary.

  □ If you omitted the ASSIGN statement or specified it with a NO value, you must resolve any duplicate SAS variable names in the view descriptor. You can use the UNIQUE statement to automatically generate unique names, or you can use the RENAME statement to resolve these duplicate names yourself. See the RENAME statement earlier in this chapter for information on it.

  If duplicate SAS variable names exist in the access descriptor on which you are creating a view descriptor, you can specify the UNIQUE statement to resolve the duplication. You specify the YES (or Y) value to have the SAS/ACCESS interface append numbers to any duplicate SAS variable names, thus making each variable name unique.

  If you specify a NO (or N) value for the UNIQUE statement, the SAS/ACCESS interface continues to allow duplicate SAS variable names to exist. You must resolve these duplicate names before saving (and thereby creating) the view descriptor.

  If you are running your SAS/ACCESS job in noninteractive or batch mode, it is recommended that you use the UNIQUE statement. If you do not and the SAS System encounters duplicate SAS variable names in a view descriptor, your job will fail.

  The equal sign (=) is optional in the UNIQUE statement. UN is the alias for this statement.

DB2 statements

In "Portable Statements" earlier in this chapter, the syntax referred to *database-identification-statements*, which are unique to each database management system supported by a SAS/ACCESS interface. The following statements are used to identify the DB2 table or DB2 view you want to use when creating an access descriptor.

All database-identification statements must immediately follow the CREATE statement that specifies the access descriptor to be created. The order of the database-identification statements does not matter. For example, you could issue either the SSID= or the TABLE= statement first. Database-identification statements are only required if you are creating access descriptors. Because DBMS information is stored in an access descriptor, you do not need to repeat this information when creating view descriptors.

The SAS/ACCESS interface to DB2 uses the following statements in interactive line, noninteractive, or batch mode:

SSID =*subsystem-id*;
> specifies the DB2 subsystem ID to use for the access descriptor. The SSID= statement is optional and is limited to four characters in length. If you omit it, the SAS System connects to the default DB2 subsystem specified by the DB2SSID= SAS system option.

TABLE = <*authorization-id.*>*table-name*;
> identifies the DB2 table or DB2 view you want to use to create an access descriptor. If you do not specify an authorization ID in interactive line or noninteractive mode, it defaults to your TSO (or MVS) userid. In batch mode, you must specify an authorization ID or an error message will be generated. The TABLE= statement is required.

ORACLE statements

In "Portable Statements" earlier in this chapter, the syntax referred to *database-identification-statements*, which are unique to each database management system supported by a SAS/ACCESS interface. The following statements are used to identify the ORACLE table or ORACLE view you want to use when creating an access descriptor.

All database-identification statements must immediately follow the CREATE statement that specifies the access descriptor to be created. The order of the database-identification statements does not matter. For example, you could issue either the ORACLEPW= or the USER= statement first. Database-identification statements are only required if you are creating access descriptors. Because DBMS information is stored in an access descriptor, you do not need to repeat this information when creating view descriptors.

The SAS/ACCESS interface to ORACLE uses the following statements in interactive line, noninteractive, or batch mode:

USER =*ORACLE-username*;
> specifies the ORACLE username to use to execute the procedure. The USER= statement is optional. If you omit an ORACLE username and password, the ORACLE default logon ID OPS$*sysid* is used.

ORACLEPW = *ORACLE-password*;
 specifies an optional ORACLE password. If you omit an ORACLE username
 and password, the ORACLE default logon ID OPS$*sysid* is used. ORAPW= is
 the alias for the ORACLEPW= statement.

TABLE = <'>*ORACLE-tablename*<'>;
 specifies the name of the ORACLE table or ORACLE view you want to use to
 create an access descriptor. If the table name contains blanks or special
 characters, you must enclose the name in quotes. The TABLE= statement is
 required.

PATH = '*ORACLE-path-designation-field*';
 specifies the ORACLE two-task device driver, database, and multi-row buffer
 size to use to retrieve data from ORACLE tables or ORACLE views on a local
 or remote ORACLE system. The PATH= statement is optional; see below for
 information on its default value.
 The format of the *ORACLE-path-designation-field* argument is as follows:

'@*driver_prefix*:*driver_and_db_parameters*,BUFFSIZE=*buffer_size*';

 The *driver_prefix* argument is the two-task device driver you want to use.
 An at sign (@) is required before this argument and a colon (:) after this
 argument. In Release 6.07 of the SAS System running under the VMS
 operating system, you can use the following values in the *driver_prefix*
 argument:

2   specifies the VMS mailbox driver used to access a database on the local
    system

D   specifies the DECnet network services driver to access a local or
    remote database

A   specifies the ORACLE asynchronous protocol

T   specifies the TCP/IP protocol.

 The *driver_and_db_parameters* are driver-specific qualifiers. See the
 ORACLE documentation on each two-task device driver for information on
 these parameters and qualifiers.
 The BUFFSIZE= argument is a user option for specifying the multi-row
 buffer size (or fetch interval) to be used when retrieving data from an
 ORACLE table or view. It enables you to specify a desired buffer size; its
 default value is 25 rows. A comma must separate BUFFSIZE= from the
 previous argument.
 The ACCESS procedure stores the specified BUFFSIZE= value when it
 creates an access descriptor. View descriptors based on this access descriptor
 retain the BUFFSIZE= value in the descriptor portion of the view.
 The PATH= statement is optional. If you omit this statement, the
 following default value is used for the VMS operating system:

```
path='@2:512,buffsize=25';
```

 This default assumes the VMS mailbox two-task driver has a mailbox size of
 512 bytes and a multi-row buffer size of 25 rows.
 You can also enter the information provided by the PATH= statement
 before invoking the SAS System under the VMS operating system. You can
 enter the DCL DEFINE command with the SASORA_PATH logical name from

the VMS prompt. The syntax for the SASORA_PATH logical name is similar
to that of the PATH= statement:

DEFINE SASORA_PATH '@*driver_prefix:driver_and_db_parameters*
     ,BUFFSIZE=*buffer_size*'

The PATH= statement and SASORA_PATH logical name are processed in
the following order of precedence:

1. If the PATH= statement is defined, the SAS System uses the specifications
    in the PATH= statement even if the SASORA_PATH logical name is
    defined.

2. If the PATH= statement is not defined, the SAS System uses the
    specifications in the SASORA_PATH logical name.

3. If neither the PATH= statement nor the SASORA_PATH logical name is
    defined, the SAS System defaults to the VMS two-task mailbox driver.

If your site already uses the ORA_DFLT_HOSTSTR logical name to
define driver specifications, you can take advantage of this by equating
SASORA_PATH to this logical name, as in the following:

```
DEFINE SASORA_PATH  ORA_DFLT_HOSTSTR
```

Rdb/VMS Statements

In "Portable Statements" earlier in this chapter, the syntax referred to
database-identification-statements, which are unique to each database management
system supported by a SAS/ACCESS interface. The following statements are used
to identify the Rdb/VMS table or Rdb/VMS view you want to use when creating
an access descriptor.

All database-identification statements must immediately follow the CREATE
statement that specifies the access descriptor to be created. The order of the
database-identification statements does not matter. For example, you could issue
either the DATABASE= or the TABLE= statement first. Database-identification
statements are only required if you are creating access descriptors. Because DBMS
information is stored in an access descriptor, you do not need to repeat this
information when creating view descriptors.

The SAS/ACCESS interface to Rdb/VMS uses the following statements in
interactive line, noninteractive, or batch mode:

DATABASE= <'>*database*<'>;
    indicates the name and physical location of the database that you want to use.
    This name can be a fully qualified VMS pathname of the database or a VMS
    logical name that refers to a database. The .RDB file extension in the database
    name is optional. Include a node name in the database name if you want to
    retrieve Rdb/VMS data in a remote database.

    The DATABASE= statement is optional if you have defined a default
    database with the SQL$DATABASE logical name. In this case, the CONNECT
    statement connects to the default database. If you have not defined a default
    database, you must include the DATABASE= statement.

    When creating multiple access descriptors in one PROC ACCESS
    execution, you only need to specify one DATABASE= statement if all the
    Rdb/VMS tables or views specified when creating subsequent access

descriptors (using TABLE= statements) are contained in the same database. That is, the subsequent access descriptors default to the database specified with the DATABASE= statement and not to the default database specified with the SQL$DATABASE logical name. To switch to another database, just specify another DATABASE= statement in your next access descriptor.

TABLE= <'>*table-name*<'>;
specifies the name of the table you want to use to create an access descriptor. If the table name contains blanks or special characters, you must enclose it in quotes. The TABLE= statement is required.

SQL/DS Statements

In "Portable Statements" earlier in this chapter, the syntax referred to *database-identification-statements*, which are unique to each database management system supported by a SAS/ACCESS interface. The following statements are used to identify the SQL/DS table or SQL/DS view you want to use when creating an access descriptor.

All database-identification statements must immediately follow the CREATE statement that specifies the access descriptor to be created. The order of the database-identification statements does not matter. For example, you could issue either the SQLDSPW or the TABLE= statement first. Database-identifcation statements are only required if you are creating access descriptors. Because DBMS information is stored in an access descriptor, you do not need to repeat this information when creating view descriptors.

The SAS/ACCESS interface to SQL/DS uses the following statements in interactive line, noninteractive, or batch mode:

SQLDSPW<=>*SQL/DS-password*;
specifies the SQL/DS password connected to the SQL/DS userid specified in the USER statement. The SQLDSPW statement is optional; however, if you specify the SQLDSPW statement, you must also specify the USER statement.

TABLE= <'><*authorization-id.*>*table-name*<'>;
specifies the name of the SQL/DS table or SQL/DS view you want to use to create an access descriptor. If you omit an authorization ID, it defaults to your SQL/DS userid. The TABLE= statement is required.

If the authorization ID or table name contains blanks or special characters, you must enclose the entire name in quotes.

USER<=>*SQL/DS-user-name*;
specifies the SQL/DS userid that corresponds to the authorization ID, or owner, of the table. If you omit the USER statement, the userid defaults to your SQL/DS userid. The USER statement is necessary when the SQL/DS userid running PROC ACCESS is not the same as the SQL/DS userid that created the table. It provides the necessary connection to the SQL/DS userid. The USER statement is optional; however, if you specify the USER statement, you must also specify the SQLDSPW statement.

Referential Integrity for the DB2 and SQL/DS Interfaces

IBM has implemented referential integrity in the DB2 and SQL/DS database management systems by specifying conditions where all references from one database column to another column must be validated.

These referential constraints are established by defining primary keys and foreign keys for the columns in the relationship. A primary key defines a unique identifier for the rows of a table and a foreign key is a column where each value contains a value in the primary key. Once the relationship between a primary key and a foreign key has been established, DB2 and SQL/DS enforce the referential integrity for you according to the rules they have established and the referential constraints you have specified.

One of these rules affects users of the SAS/ACCESS interfaces to DB2 and SQL/DS. You cannot update a primary key using the WHERE CURRENT OF clause in an UPDATE statement. The SAS/ACCESS interface view engines for DB2 and SQL/DS use this type of update call to perform updates. To allow you to update other columns of a table with a primary key, the SAS/ACCESS engines for DB2 and SQL/DS have been modified to determine which columns make up the primary key so that these columns can be omitted from the UPDATE statement. Changes to the primary key are ignored and any other changes to data in the row are made.

Examples

This section presents some examples of creating access descriptors and view descriptors using the PROC ACCESS options and statements described previously.

You can submit these examples in a SAS program from the PROGRAM EDITOR window, one line at a time in interactive line mode, or surround the program with the appropriate operating system statements and submit the job in batch mode.

Creating Access and View Descriptors in One PROC Step

Perhaps the most common way to use the ACCESS procedure is to create an access descriptor and one or more view descriptors in a single PROC ACCESS execution.

The following example creates an access descriptor MYLIB.INVOICE based on the DB2 table SASDEMO.INVOICE. Two view descriptors are created, VLIB.EXCHRATE and VLIB.NOPAYMT, based on this access descriptor. Each SAS/ACCESS statement is then explained in the order it appears in the example program.

```
proc access dbms=db2;
   create mylib.invoice.access;
      table=sasdemo.invoice;
      assign=yes;
      rename invoicenum=invnum amtbilled=amtbilld amountinus=amtusa
         computedexchange=compexch;
```

```
            format amtbilled dollar18.2 amountinus dollar18.2;
            list all;

         create vlib.exchrate.view;
            select invoicenum billedon billedto country amtbilled
               computedexchange amountinus;
         create vlib.nopaymt.view;
            select invoicenum billedto amountinus billedon;
            subset where country='USA' and paidon is null;
      run;
```

Here is an explanation of the statements in this example:

proc access dbms=db2;
    invokes the ACCESS procedure for the SAS/ACCESS interface to DB2.

create mylib.invoice.access;
    identifies the access descriptor, MYLIB.INVOICE, that you want to create. The MYLIB libref must be associated with a SAS data library before you can specify it in this statement.

table=sasdemo.invoice;
    indicates the access descriptor is to be created from the DB2 table named INVOICE, which has the authorization ID name SASDEMO.

assign=yes;
    generates unique SAS variable names from the first eight characters of the DB2 column names. SAS variable formats are generated automatically from the columns' SQL data types. These variable names and formats can be changed in this access descriptor but not in any view descriptors created from this access descriptor.

rename invoicenum=invnum amtbilled=amtbilld
    amountinus=amtusa computedexchange=compexch;
    renames the SAS variables associated with the INVOICENUM, AMTBILLED, AMOUNTINUS, and COMPUTEDEXCHANGE columns. Because the ASSIGN=YES statement is specified, any view descriptors created from this access descriptor automatically use the new SAS variable names.

format amtbilled dollar18.2 amountinus dollar18.2;
    assigns the SAS format DOLLAR18.2 to the SAS variables associated with the AMTBILLED and AMOUNTINUS columns. Notice that you specify the DB2 column names in this statement. Because the ASSIGN=YES statement is specified, any view descriptors created from this access descriptor automatically use the new SAS variable formats. Using an equal sign (=) in this statement is optional.

list all;
    lists the access descriptor's columns, variables, and formats; in noninteractive or batch mode, the list is written to the SAS log. Any columns that have been dropped from display (using the DROP statement) are not listed.

create vlib.exchrate.view;
    writes the previous access descriptor and identifies the view descriptor, VLIB.EXCHRATE, that you want to create. The VLIB libref must be associated with a SAS data library before you can specify it in this statement.

```
select invoicenum billedon billedto country amtbilled
    computedexchange amountinus;
```
selects the INVOICENUM, BILLEDON, BILLEDTO, COUNTRY, AMTBILLED, COMPUTEDEXCHANGE, and AMOUNTINUS columns for inclusion in a view descriptor. The SELECT statement is required to create the view. Notice that you specify the DB2 column names in this statement.

```
create vlib.nopaymt.view;
```
writes the previous view descriptor and identifies the next view descriptor, VLIB.NOPAYMT, that you want to create.

```
select invoicenum billedto amountinus billedon;
```
selects the INVOICENUM, BILLEDTO, AMOUNTINUS, and BILLEDON columns for inclusion in a view descriptor.

```
subset where country='USA' and paidon is null;
```
specifies you want the view descriptor to include only observations for companies based in the U.S. who have not paid their bills yet. Notice that you specify the DB2 SQL WHERE clause syntax and column names in this statement.

```
run;
```
writes the last view descriptor when the RUN statement is processed.

Creating Only Access Descriptors

You use the CREATE statement in the ACCESS procedure to create access descriptors. You can either create a single access descriptor or several access descriptors in the same procedure execution.

Creating a Single Access Descriptor

The following example creates a single access descriptor, MYLIB.EMPLOYEE, based on the SQL/DS SASDEMO.EMPLOYEES table. Each SAS/ACCESS statement is then explained in the order it appears in the example program.

```
proc access dbms=sqlds;
    create mylib.employ.access;
        table=sasdemo.employees;
        drop salary;
        rename lastname=lname firstname=fname middlename=mname;
        format hiredate date9. birthdate date9.;
        list;
run;
```

Here is an explanation of the statements in this example:

```
proc access dbms=sqlds;
```
invokes the ACCESS procedure for the SAS/ACCESS interface to SQL/DS.

```
create mylib.employ.access;
```
identifies the access descriptor, MYLIB.EMPLOY, that you want to create. Descriptor names are limited to seven characters in the SQL/DS interface. The MYLIB libref must be associated with a SAS data library before you can specify it in this statement.

```
table=sasdemo.employees;
```
indicates the access descriptor is created from the SQL/DS table named
EMPLOYEES, which has the authorization ID name SASDEMO.

```
drop salary;
```
marks the SALARY column as non-display. Therefore, the SALARY column
does not appear in any view descriptor created from this access descriptor.

```
rename lastname=lname firstname=fname middlename=mname;
```
renames the SAS variables associated with the LASTNAME, FIRSTNAME, and
MIDDLENAME columns. The equal sign (=) is optional.

```
format hiredate date9. birthdate date9.;
```
assigns the SAS format DATE9. to the SAS variables associated with the
HIREDATE and BIRTHDATE columns. Notice that you specify the SQL/DS
column names in this statement.

```
list;
```
lists the access descriptor's columns, variables, and formats; in noninteractive
or batch mode, the list is written to the SAS log. Any columns that have been
dropped from display (using the DROP statement) are listed with the
NON-DISPLAY characteristic.

```
run;
```
writes the access descriptor when the RUN statement is processed.

Creating Several Access Descriptors

You can create several access descriptors in one execution of the ACCESS
procedure. The following example creates two access descriptors,
MYLIB.NEWHIRES and MYLIB.FIVEYEAR, from two separate Rdb/VMS views.
Each SAS/ACCESS statement is then explained in the order it appears in the
example code.

```
proc access dbms=rdb;
    create mylib.newhires.access;
        database='qa:[schwartz]personnel';
        table=newhires;
        assign=yes;
        drop phone;
        rename middlename=midname beginning_salary=beginpay;
        format hiredate=date9. birthdate=date9. beginning_salary=dollar12.2;
    create mylib.fiveyear.access;
        table=fiveyears;
        assign=no;
        format hiredate=date9. birthdate=date9.
           beginning_salary=dollar12.2 current_salary=dollar12.2;
    run;
```

Here is an explanation of the statements in this example:

```
proc access dbms=rdb;
```
invokes the ACCESS procedure for the SAS/ACCESS interface to Rdb/VMS.

```
create mylib.newhires.access;
```
identifies the access descriptor, MYLIB.NEWHIRES, that you want to create. The MYLIB libref must be associated with a SAS data library before you can specify it in this statement.

```
database='qa:[schwartz]personnel';
table=newhires;
```
identifies the database containing the Rdb/VMS table or view on which the access descriptor is to be based. If you have defined a default database with the SQL$DATABASE logical name and you want to use that database, you can omit the DATABASE= statement. In this example, the TABLE= statement specifies the Rdb/VMS view, NEWHIRES.

```
assign=yes;
```
generates unique SAS variable names from the first eight characters of the Rdb/VMS column names. SAS variable formats are generated automatically from the database columns' data types. These variable names and formats can be changed in this access descriptor but not in any view descriptors created from this access descriptor.

```
drop phone;
```
marks the PHONE column as non-display. Therefore, the PHONE column does not appear in any view descriptor created from this access descriptor.

```
rename middlename=midname beginning_salary=beginpay;
```
renames the SAS variables associated with the MIDDLENAME and BEGINNING_SALARY columns. Because the ASSIGN=YES statement is specified, any view descriptors created from this access descriptor automatically use the new SAS variable names. Using the equal sign (=) in this statement is optional.

```
format hiredate=date9. birthdate=date9.
   beginning_salary=dollar12.2;
```
assigns the SAS format DATE9. to the SAS variables associated with the HIREDATE and BIRTHDATE columns and the DOLLAR12.2 format to the BEGINNING_SALARY column. Notice that you specify the Rdb/VMS column names in this statement. Because the ASSIGN=YES statement is specified, any view descriptors created from this access descriptor automatically use the new SAS variable formats.

```
create mylib.fiveyear.access;
```
writes the first access descriptor and identifies another access descriptor (MYLIB.FIVEYEAR) that you want to create.

```
table=fiveyears;
```
identifies another Rdb/VMS view, FIVEYEARS, which is contained in the QA:[SCHWARTZ]PERSONNEL database. Once a DATABASE= statement is included in a PROC ACCESS step, the SAS System assumes that DBMS tables or views specified in subsequent access descriptors are contained in this same database.

```
assign=no;
```
generates SAS variable names based on the first eight characters of the Rdb/VMS column names, although the names are not displayed even if you use the LIST statement. SAS variable formats are also generated based on the columns' database types. These variable names and formats can be changed in the access descriptor and in any view descriptors created from this access

(assign = continued)

descriptor. You must resolve any duplicate variable names when creating the views.

```
format hiredate=date9. birthdate=date9.
   beginning_salary=dollar12.2 current_salary=dollar12.2;
```
assigns the DATE9. format to the SAS variables associated with the HIREDATE and BIRTHDATE columns and assigns the DOLLAR12.2 format to the variables associated with the BEGINNING_SALARY and CURRENT_SALARY columns. You specify the Rdb/VMS column names in this statement. Using an equal sign (=) is optional. Because the ASSIGN=NO statement is specified, you can change the formats in any view descriptor created from this access descriptor.

```
run;
```
writes the last access descriptor when the RUN statement is processed.

Creating Only View Descriptors

To use the ACCESS procedure to create only view descriptors, invoke the procedure with the ACCDESC= option. You can create one or more view descriptors in the same procedure execution.

Creating a Single View Descriptor

You can use the ACCESS procedure to create a view descriptor from an existing access descriptor, as in the following example using the SAS/ACCESS interface to ORACLE. This example creates a view descriptor named VLIB.OLDCUST from an access descriptor named MYLIB.CUSTOMER. Each SAS/ACCESS statement is then explained in the order it appears in the example program.

```
proc access dbms=oracle accdesc=mylib.customer;
   create vlib.oldcust.view;
      unique=yes;
      select customer name firstorderdate telephone;
      subset where firstorderdate < '01-JUN-80';
run;
```

No database-identification statements are required in this example because the DBMS information is stored in the access descriptor. Here is an explanation of the statements in this example:

```
proc access dbms=oracle accdesc=mylib.customer;
```
invokes the ACCESS procedure for the SAS/ACCESS interface to ORACLE and specifies that the view descriptor will be created based on the access descriptor MYLIB.CUSTOMER. The MYLIB libref must be associated with a SAS data library before you can specify it in the ACCDESC= option.

```
create vlib.oldcust.view;
```
identifies the view descriptor, VLIB.OLDCUST, that you want to create. The VLIB libref must be associated with a SAS data library before you can specify it in this statement.

```
unique=yes;
```
specifies unique SAS variable names are generated for columns that are selected for the view descriptor. You can only use this statement if you have omitted the ASSIGN statement (or specified a NO value) when creating the access descriptor on which this view is based.

```
select customer name firstorderdate telephone;
```
selects four columns for the view descriptor. The SELECT statement is required to create the view. You specify the ORACLE column names in this statement.

```
subset where firstorderdate < '01-JUN-80';
```
specifies you only want the view descriptor to include observations where the FIRSTORDERDATE contains a date earlier than June 01, 1980. You specify the ORACLE SQL WHERE clause syntax and column names in this statement.

```
run;
```
writes the view descriptor when the RUN statement is processed.

Creating Several View Descriptors

You can create more than one view descriptor in a single PROC ACCESS execution. The following example uses the SAS/ACCESS interface to ORACLE to create two view descriptors, named VLIB.GOLDORD and VLIB.ASBESTOS. Each SAS/ACCESS statement is then explained in the order it appears in the example program.

```
proc access dbms=oracle accdesc=mylib.orders(alter=gelb);
    create vlib.goldord.view;
        select ordernum length shipto takenby;
        reset fabriccharges;
        rename fabriccharges fabcharg;
        subset where stocknum=8934;
        list all;
    create vlib.asbestos.view;
        select ordernum shipto fabriccharges dateordered;
        subset where stocknum=1279 and processedby is null;
        list view;
run;
```

No database-identification statements are required in this example, because the DBMS information is stored in the access descriptor. Here is an explanation of the statements in this example:

```
proc access dbms=oracle accdesc=mylib.orders(alter=gelb);
```
invokes the ACCESS procedure for the SAS/ACCESS interface to ORACLE and specifies that the view descriptors will be created based on the access descriptor MYLIB.ORDERS. The MYLIB libref must be associated with a SAS data library before you can specify it in the ACCDESC= option.

Using the SAS data set option ALTER= is required when creating view descriptors based on the MYLIB.ORDERS access descriptor, because this access descriptor has an ALTER-level password assigned to it.

`create vlib.goldord.view;`
identifies the view descriptor, VLIB.GOLDORD, that you want to create. The VLIB libref must be associated with a SAS data library before you can specify it in this statement.

`select ordernum length shipto takenby;`
selects four columns for the view descriptor. Because the FABRICCHARGES column is specified in the RENAME statement, it is also selected. The SELECT statement is required and you specify ORACLE column names in this statement.

`reset fabriccharges;`
resets the FABRICCHARGES column to its defaults values (that is, the SAS variable name based on the first eight characters of the ORACLE column name and the SAS format based on the ORACLE data type). You specify the ORACLE column names in this statement. You can only change a view's variable names and formats if the ASSIGN statement has been omitted or given a NO value when its access descriptor was created.

`rename fabriccharges fabcharg;`
renames the SAS variable associated with the FABRICCHARGES column. (This column continues to use the default SAS format reset by the RESET statement because this default is not modified with a FORMAT= statement.)

`subset where stocknum=8934;`
specifies you want the view descriptor to include only observations in which the STOCKNUM is 8934, which is the stock number. You specify ORACLE SQL WHERE clause syntax and column names in the SUBSET statement.

`list all;`
lists all the available positional equivalents, DBMS column names, SAS variable names, and SAS formats in the access descriptor on which the view is based; columns that have been dropped from the access descriptor are not listed. Selection criteria specified in the view descriptor are listed. Columns that have been selected for the view have *SELECTED* next to them. In noninteractive and batch modes, the list is written to the SAS log.

`create vlib.asbestos.view;`
writes the previous view descriptor and identifies the next view descriptor, VLIB.ASBESTOS, that you want to create.

`select ordernum shipto fabriccharges dateordered;`
selects four columns for the view descriptor. This view uses the SAS variable name for the FABRICCHARGES column that is specified in the access descriptor, MYLIB.ORDERS, even though this column was reset and renamed in the previously created view, VLIB.GOLDORD. Variable names in a view descriptor are always based on those in the access descriptor, even if other views are created in the same PROC ACCESS execution.

`subset where stocknum=1279 and processedby is null;`
specifies you want the view descriptor to include only observations in which the STOCKNUM is 1279 and the PROCESSEDBY value is null (that is, the order has not yet been processed).

`list view;`
lists the positional equivalents, DBMS column names, SAS variable names, and SAS formats that have been selected for the view descriptor. Selection criteria specified for the view are also listed. In noninteractive and batch modes, the list is written to the SAS log.

`run;`
writes the last view descriptor when the RUN statement is processed.

Commands

The following section describes the commands that can be issued in the ACCESS window and in the View Descriptor Display window. The commands fall into two types:

□ command-line commands

□ selection-field commands.

There is also a new command, the SELECTALL command, that can be issued in the View Descriptor Display window.

For ease of use, the following command-line and selection-field commands are listed alphabetically.

Command-line Commands for the ACCESS Window

The following commands are valid on the ACCESS window command line:

BACKWARD | UP   scrolls the display backward. UP is the alias for BACKWARD.

BOTTOM   scrolls to the end of the list of SAS files contained in the window.

CANCEL | END   exits the ACCESS procedure. END is the alias for CANCEL.

COPY   copies a member of a SAS data library to another data library. The syntax for this command is

COPY <*source_libref.*>*member*<*.type*> <*destination_libref.*>*member*<*.type*>

The *libref* argument refers to the SAS data library where the *member* is stored. The *member* argument can be the name of an access descriptor, a catalog, a SAS data set, or a stored program of member *type* ACCESS, CATALOG, DATA, PROGRAM, or VIEW.

(COPY continued)

A one-level name assumes WORK as the libref and DATA as the member type (unless a default libref or type has been set up with the LIBRARY and MEMTYPE commands, respectively). WORK refers to the SAS System's default temporary data library. A two-level name assumes a type of DATA.

The _ALL_ keyword can be used as the member name or type to copy a group of members. For example, to copy all SAS data sets (of type DATA) from the library MYLIB to the library NEWLIB, you would use:

```
copy mylib._all_.data  newlib
```

If the destination member or library already exists, use the REPLACE command, described later in this section.

You can use the COPY command to copy the data accessed by a SAS data view into a SAS data file (that is, extract the view's data). The following example copies data accessed by a view descriptor into a new SAS data file:

```
copy vlib.usacust.view  mydata.usacust.data
```

If the SAS data view is password-protected, the same password and level of protection apply to the new SAS data file. You do not specify the password when copying the SAS data view, but you may need to supply the password when using the SAS data file, depending on the kind of SAS data view copied and its level of protection. For example, if a READ password is assigned to a view descriptor and you copy its data to a SAS data file, you must supply the password before you are allowed to browse the data in the new data file.

CREATE
creates an access descriptor in display manager mode using windows. The syntax for this command is

CREATE *libref.access-descriptor.*ACCESS

The *libref.access-descriptor.*ACCESS argument is the three-level name that specifies the libref, member name, and member type of ACCESS for the descriptor you want to create. The libref is required in this command. If you want to create a temporary access descriptor, use the libref WORK, which refers to the SAS System's default temporary data library.

EXTRACT
extracts data described by a view descriptor, PROC SQL view, or DATA step view and places them in a SAS data file. The syntax for this command is

EXTRACT <*libref.*>*view-name* <*libref.*>*SAS-data-file*

The *libref.view-name* argument specifies a two-level name (libref and member name) for the view that describes the data you want to extract. The *libref.SAS-data-file* argument specifies a two-level name (libref and member name) for the output SAS data file. If you want to create a temporary data file, use the libref WORK, which refers to the SAS System's default temporary data library.

FORWARD | DOWN   scrolls the display forward. DOWN is the alias for FORWARD.

HELP   obtains help from the SAS System.

LABEL   adds a column to the ACCESS window that displays any SAS data set labels specified using the LABEL= data set option; entering LABEL again removes the labels column from the display.

LIBRARY   limits the display to a particular libref. The syntax for this command is

LIBRARY *libref* | _ALL_

ALL displays all librefs; _ALL_ is the window's default display.

LOAD   invokes the DBLOAD procedure in display manager mode and opens the Engine Selection window. This command enables you to use windows to load a SAS data set into a DBMS table. You can specify an optional *DBMS-name* argument to bypass the Engine Selection window and open the DBLOAD Identification window. The syntax for this command is

LOAD <*DBMS-name*>

MEMTYPE   limits the display to a member type, for example DATA or CATALOG. The syntax for this command is

MEMTYPE *type* | _ALL_

ALL displays all members; _ALL_ is the window's default display.

REPLACE   copies a member of a SAS data library to another data library, overwriting the destination member if it exists. The syntax for this command is

REPLACE <*source_libref.*>*name*<*.type*>
           <*destination_libref.*>*name*<*.type*>

The REPLACE command uses the same arguments and defaults as the COPY command; refer to its description earlier in this section for more information.

RESET   redisplays the window. The RESET command resets the library and member types to display all members; it also displays any new members that have been created.

SORT   sorts the display in descending alphabetical order. The syntax for this command is

(SORT continued)

> SORT *argument-1* <*argument-n*>
>
> The values for *argument* can be LIBREF, NAME, and MEMTYPE. The second argument is used when you want to sort within the first argument. Initially, the display is sorted by library and then by member types.

TOP
> scrolls to the top of the list of SAS files contained in the window.

Selection-field Commands for the ACCESS Window

The following selection-field commands are available in the ACCESS window. Type a selection-field command in the field in front of the appropriate member and press the ENTER key. All the commands are listed in alphabetic order for ease of use.

Note in the command descriptions that a *SAS data view* can include a view descriptor, PROC SQL view, or DATA step view; references to a *SAS data set* can include a SAS data view and a SAS data file.

B*
> (browse data)
> can be placed by a SAS data set. It enables you to use the FSBROWSE procedure to browse the data in a SAS data file or the data described by a SAS data view. The B command is equivalent to invoking the FSBROWSE procedure in display manager mode or in interactive line mode with the appropriate DATA= option. With this command you see only one observation of data at a time.
>
> Before you can browse data retrieved through a SAS/ACCESS interface, you must be granted privileges by the DBMS. See your Release 6.06 SAS/ACCESS documentation for more information.

BD
> (browse descriptor)
> can be placed by either an access descriptor or a view descriptor. It enables you to browse the descriptor's columns, SAS names, formats, and so on. For access and view descriptors, columns dropped from the display are not listed.
>
> To browse the view descriptor, you do not need read-privileges on the access descriptor that was used to create the view descriptor.

BL*
> (browse listing)
> can be placed by a SAS data set. It enables you to use the FSVIEW procedure to browse the data in a tabular listing similar to that produced by the PRINT procedure. The BL command is equivalent to invoking the FSVIEW procedure in display manager mode or in interactive line mode with the appropriate DATA= option and no MODIFY option specified.

This selection-field command requires SAS/FSP software as well as SAS/ACCESS software.

Before you can browse data retrieved through a SAS/ACCESS interface, you must be granted privileges by the DBMS. See your Release 6.06 SAS/ACCESS documentation for more information.

C (contents)

can be placed by a SAS data set. It enables you to browse descriptive information about a SAS data view or browse and edit descriptive information in a SAS data file. This information is similar to what is produced by the CONTENTS procedure.

When you place the C selection-field command next to a SAS data view, the CONTENTS window appears in browse mode. When you place the C command next to a SAS data file, the CONTENTS window appears in edit mode if you have write access to the library. In edit mode, you can type over variable names, formats, informats, and labels to change the current values. To browse or edit additional descriptive information about the SAS data set, move the cursor to the Data Set Attributes field and press ENTER. The Attributes window appears and displays information such as the data set name, engine, date created, date last modified, data set label, and number of observations.

You can issue the following commands in the CONTENTS window:

INDEX CREATE

opens the Index Create window, enabling you to create indexes on variables in the displayed SAS data file. (Refer to Chapter 6 in *SAS Language: Reference, Version 6, First Edition* for more information on SAS indexes.) This command is valid only if the CONTENTS window is opened for editing. You cannot use this command with a SAS data view.

You can issue the following commands in the Index Create window:

END   closes the Index Create window.

REVIEW   opens the Index Review window to display the SAS indexes already defined for this SAS data file. You can also delete existing indexes in this window.

RUN   creates an index on one or more variables after all required information has been specified.

INDEX REVIEW

opens the Index Review window so that you can view the SAS indexes currently defined for the SAS data file. This command is valid only if the CONTENTS window is opened for editing. You can use the D selection-field command in this window to delete any of the listed indexes. You cannot use this command with a SAS data view.

SORT <NAME | ORDER>

sorts the variables in the CONTENTS window display; this command affects only the variables' display and not their actual order in a SAS data set. By default, variables are listed in the order they are defined in the SAS data set. Specifying SORT NAME sorts the display by variable names in descending alphabetical order. Specifying SORT

(C continued)

ORDER (or SORT alone) restores the original order. This command is valid in the CONTENTS window for any SAS data set.

CV   (create view)
can be placed by an access descriptor. It enables you to create a view descriptor based on this access descriptor in display manager mode using windows.

D   (delete member)
can be placed by any member in the ACCESS window. It enables you to delete that member. Enter a V and press ENTER at the verification request to complete the deletion. If you do not enter a V, the request to delete is canceled.

This command deletes the SAS data set or SAS/ACCESS descriptor, not the descriptor's underlying DBMS table or view.

E*   (edit data)
can be placed by a view descriptor or SAS data file. It enables you to use the FSEDIT procedure to edit DBMS data (via the view descriptor) or to edit the data in a SAS data file. The E command is equivalent to invoking the FSEDIT procedure in display manager mode or in interactive line mode with the appropriate DATA= option. With this command, you see only one observation of data at a time.

Before you can update data retrieved through a SAS/ACCESS interface, you must be granted privileges by the DBMS. See your Release 6.06 SAS/ACCESS documentation for more information.

ED   (edit descriptor)
can be placed by an access descriptor or view descriptor. It enables you to edit the descriptor's SAS variable names, formats, and so on, to select or drop columns, and to change selection criteria. Whether you can change SAS names and formats in the view descriptor depends on the value you gave the ASSIGN statement (in interactive line, noninteractive, or batch mode) or the Assign Names field in the Access Descriptor Identification window (in display manager mode).

EL*   (edit listing)
can be placed by a view descriptor or SAS data file. It enables you to use the FSVIEW procedure to edit the data in a tabular listing similar to that produced by the PRINT procedure. When using the EL command next to a view descriptor, you are directly updating DBMS data in a SAS data file. The EL command is equivalent to invoking the FSVIEW procedure in display manager mode or in interactive line mode with the appropriate DATA= option and the MODIFY option specified.

Before you can update data retrieved through a SAS/ACCESS interface, you must be granted privileges by the DBMS. See your Release 6.06 SAS/ACCESS documentation for more information.

This selection-field command requires SAS/FSP software as well as SAS/ACCESS software.

PW   (password)
     can be placed by an access or view descriptor, a SAS data set, or a
     program (member of type PROGRAM) and enables you to assign it an
     ALTER, READ, or WRITE password.

     When you enter the PW command, a window appears prompting you
     to enter or change a password. New passwords are not displayed as you
     enter them nor are existing passwords displayed. Issue the END
     command to save the passwords and return to the ACCESS window.

     Note: You must write down or store your passwords elsewhere,
     because you cannot retrieve them from the SAS System.

     When a password-protected SAS data set or stored DATA step
     program is used in a SAS program, the data set's password may need to
     be specified by using a SAS data set option, depending on the PW type
     and the access type, or you will be prompted if you are running the
     procedure interactively. See "Specifying SAS System Passwords for
     SAS/ACCESS Descriptors" later in this chapter and SAS Technical Report
     P-222, *Changes and Enhancements to Base SAS Software, Release 6.07* for
     more information on and examples of using passwords.

R   (rename member)
     can be placed by any member and enables you to rename that member.
     Press ENTER, type the new name over the existing member name, and
     press ENTER again. This command renames the data set or descriptor,
     not the descriptor's underlying table or view.

▶ *Caution.* . . . . *Be careful when you rename an access descriptor, because the view*
descriptors associated with it are no longer linked to it. ▲

?   can be placed by any member. It displays a window that describes all the
     selection-field commands and enables you to select any of the
     selection-field commands.

Command-line Command for the View Descriptor Display Window

A new command, the SELECTALL command, can now be issued from the View
Descriptor Display window. The SELECTALL command enables you to select all
database columns for your view descriptor.

Specifying SAS System Passwords for SAS/ACCESS Descriptors

Release 6.07 of the SAS System enables you to control access to SAS data sets and
access descriptors by associating one or more SAS System passwords with them.
You can assign a password to a descriptor by using the ACCESS window in
display manager mode or by using the DATASETS procedure. For either method,
you must first create the descriptor.

Note: In the ACCESS procedure, you cannot add a password data set option
to the CREATE statement to assign a password while a descriptor is being created.
SAS data set options are used with access and view descriptors to specify an
existing password.

Table 1.1 summarizes the levels of protection that SAS System passwords have and their effects on access descriptors and view descriptors.

Table 1.1
Password and Descriptor Interaction

Descriptor	READ=	WRITE=	ALTER=
access descriptor	no effect on descriptor	no effect on descriptor	protects descriptor from being read or edited
view descriptor	no effect on descriptor	no effect on descriptor	protects descriptor from being read or edited

For detailed information on the levels of protection and the types of passwords you can use, refer to SAS Technical Report P-222. The following section describes how you assign SAS System passwords to descriptors in the four processing modes.

Assigning Passwords

To assign a password to an access descriptor, view descriptor, or other SAS file in display manager mode, you can use the PW command in the ACCESS window. You also use this command to change passwords. The PW selection-field command is described earlier in this chapter in "Selection-field Commands for the ACCESS Window."

To assign or change a password in interactive line, noninteractive, or batch mode, you use the DATASETS procedure's MODIFY statement. Here is the basic syntax for assigning a password to an access descriptor or a view descriptor:

PROC DATASETS LIBRARY=*libref* MEMTYPE=*member-type*;
    MODIFY *descriptor-name* (*password-level*=*password-modification*);
RUN;

In this syntax statement, the *password-level* argument can have one of the following values: ALTER=, PW=, READ=, or WRITE=. The *password-modification* argument enables you to assign a new password, delete a password, or change passwords. See SAS Technical Report P-222 for all the possible combinations in this argument and for other details.

The following example assigns a password to the MYLIB.ORDERS access descriptor, which is referred to in the previous section, "Creating several view descriptors."

```
proc datasets library=mylib memtype=access;
    modify invoice(alter=gelb);
run;
```

Refer to SAS Technical Report P-222 for more examples of assigning, deleting, and using SAS System passwords.

DBLOAD Procedure

The following section describes the changes to the DBLOAD procedure for Release 6.07 of the SAS System. The procedure statements for PROC DBLOAD enable you to create and load a DBMS table using SAS data. The DBLOAD procedure also enables you to submit SQL statements to the DBMS without leaving your SAS session. The Release 6.07 changes affect only the DBLOAD procedure in the SAS/ACCESS interfaces to SQL/DS and ORACLE.

SQL/DS Interface: Procedure Statements

The DBLOAD procedure in the SAS/ACCESS interface to SQL/DS currently includes two statements, PASSWORD= and USER=. In Releases 6.06 and 6.07, the equal sign is required in these statements.

See the *SAS/ACCESS Interface to SQL/DS: Usage and Reference, Version 6, First Edition* for a description of PROC DBLOAD options and statements.

ORACLE Interface: Procedure Statements

The DBLOAD procedure in the SAS/ACCESS interface to ORACLE has a new PATH= statement, which enables you to load SAS data into an ORACLE table on a local or remote ORACLE system. There are also changes to some of the current statements used in the DBLOAD procedure, as described in the following list.

See the *SAS/ACCESS Interface to ORACLE: Usage and Reference, Version 6, First Edition* for a description of PROC DBLOAD options and statements.

USER = *ORACLE-user-name*;
  specifies the ORACLE username to be used for procedure execution. If you do not specify an ORACLE username and password, ORACLE's default userid OPS$sysid is used. The USER= and PASSWORD= statements must be specified together.

PASSWORD = *ORACLE-password*;
  specifies an ORACLE password. If you do not specify an ORACLE username and password, ORACLE's default userid OPS$sysid is used. PW= and ORAPW= are aliases for the PASSWORD= statement. The USER= and PASSWORD= statements must be specified together.

TABLE = *ORACLE-table-name*;
  specifies the name of the ORACLE table to be created and loaded with SAS data during the procedure's execution.

TABLESPACE = *ORACLE-tablespace*;
  specifies the ORACLE Version 5 SPACE or the ORACLE Version 6 TABLESPACE used to store the ORACLE table being created. SPACE= is an alias for the TABLESPACE= statement. The TABLESPACE= statement is optional.

(TABLESPACE = ORACLE-tablespace; continued)

> **Note:** This statement specifies Version 5 and Version 6 of ORACLE software, not Version 5 or Version 6 of the SAS System or SAS/ACCESS software.
> PROC DBLOAD checks to see whether the user is running ORACLE Version 5 or ORACLE Version 6 and interprets the TABLESPACE name entered as a SPACE definition or TABLESPACE definition, respectively. If nothing is specified in the TABLESPACE= statement, the new table will be loaded into the appropriate default space or tablespace. The user must be granted access by the ORACLE Database Administrator to use any space or tablespace other than the default areas.
> The ORACLE Version 5 SPACE definition and the ORACLE Version 6 TABLESPACE definition are similar but not directly synonymous, as described below.

Version 5 SPACE definition
For ORACLE Version 5, the default SPACE definition is named DEFAULT and it contains a PARTITION named SYSTEM, where user objects are stored. ORACLE Version 5 partitions are the areas set aside by ORACLE to hold user database objects such as tables, clusters, and views.

Version 6 TABLESPACE definition
For ORACLE Version 6, the default TABLESPACE definition is named SYSTEM and is the location in which user objects are stored. ORACLE Version 6 tablespaces are the areas set aside by ORACLE to hold user database objects such as tables, clusters, and views.

PATH = '*ORACLE-path-designation*';
specifies the ORACLE two-task device driver and driver-specific parameters to use to load SAS data into an ORACLE table on a local or remote ORACLE system. The PATH= statement is optional; see below for information on its default value.
The format of the *ORACLE-path-designation* argument is as follows:

'@*driver_prefix:driver_and_db_parameters*';

The *driver_prefix* argument specifies the two-task device driver you want to use. An at sign (@) is required before this argument and a colon (:) after this argument; enclose the entire argument in single quotes. In Release 6.07 of the SAS System running under the VMS operating system, you can use the following values in the *driver_prefix* argument:

2   specifies the VMS mailbox driver used to access a database on the local system.

D   specifies the DECnet network services driver to access a local or remote database.

A   specifies the ORACLE asynchronous driver to access a remote database.

T   specifies the TCP/IP driver to access a local or remote database.

The *driver_and_database_parameters* are driver-specific qualifiers. See the ORACLE documentation on each two-task device driver for information on these parameters and qualifiers.

The PATH= statement is optional. If you omit this statement, the following default value is used for the VMS operating system:

```
path='ə2:512';
```

This default assumes the VMS mailbox two-task driver has a mailbox size of 512 bytes.

You can also enter the PATH= statement before invoking the SAS System under VMS. You can enter the DCL DEFINE command with the SASORA_PATH logical name from the VMS prompt. The syntax for the SASORA_PATH logical name is similar to that of the PATH= statement:

DEFINE SASORA_PATH '@*driver_prefix:driver_and_db_parameters*'

The PATH= statement and SASORA_PATH logical name are processed in the following order of precedence:

1. If the PATH= statement is defined, the SAS/ACCESS interface to ORACLE uses the specifications in the PATH= statement even if the SASORA_PATH logical name is defined.

2. If the PATH= statement is not defined, the SAS/ACCESS interface to ORACLE uses the specifications in the SASORA_PATH logical name.

3. If neither the PATH= statement nor the SASORA_PATH logical name is defined, the SAS/ACCESS interface to ORACLE defaults to the VMS two-task mailbox driver.

If your site already uses the ORA_DFLT_HOSTSTR logical name to define driver specifications, you can take advantage of this by equating SASORA_PATH to this logical name, as in the following:

```
DEFINE SASORA_PATH  ORA_DFLT_HOSTSTR
```

PROC DBLOAD does not use the BUFFSIZE= argument.

Example

The following example loads the MONEY.RATEOFEX data set into the ORACLE table EXCHANGE. Note that the data set RATEOFEX is stored in a SAS data library that is referenced by the libref MONEY.

```
proc dbload dbms=oracle data=money.rateofex;
   user=scott;
   password=tiger;
   table=exchange;
   tablespace=system;
   path='əD:VAXNOD';
   accdesc=mylib.exchange;
   rename fgnindol=fgnindollars dolinfgn=dollarinfgn;
   nulls updated=n fgnindollars=n dollarinfgn=n country=n;
   sql grant insert on table customers to sasxyz;
```

```
        sql create view whotookorders as
            select ordernum, takenby, firstname, lastname, phone
            from orders, employees
            where orders.takenby=employees.empid;
        load;
    run;
```

Here, the PATH= statement specifies using the DECnet two-task driver to
access the default ORACLE database on VMS node VAXNOD.

Chapter **2** SAS/ACCESS® Interface to SYSTEM 2000® Data Management Software

Introduction

This chapter describes the Release 6.07 changes and enhancements in the SAS/ACCESS interfaces to SYSTEM 2000 Data Management Software, the hierarchical data management system.

With Release 6.07 of the SAS System, you can run the ACCESS procedure in interactive line, noninteractive, and batch modes, as well as in display manager mode (as described in your Release 6.06 SAS/ACCESS documentation). This flexibility enables you to choose a method for creating access descriptors and view descriptors based on your environment and personal preferences.

Also, Release 6.07 provides a SAS System password capability. You can assign passwords to access descriptors and to any kind of SAS data set. This chapter briefly describes how to assign passwords to access and view descriptors.

Syntax

This section describes the PROC ACCESS statement options and procedure statements added in Release 6.07 of the SAS System. These options enable you to run the ACCESS procedure in display manager mode or you can use the options and statements to run PROC ACCESS steps in interactive line, noninteractive, or batch mode. See "Running the SAS System" in "Using This Book" for more information on these SAS methods of operation. The syntax for creating access and view descriptors in display manager mode has not changed.

The ACCESS procedure's basic syntax for creating access and view descriptors is similar for all SAS/ACCESS products. The differences lie in the statements that you use to identify the database and in the variable attributes you specify. These differences are described later in this chapter.

Here is the basic syntax for the SYSTEM 2000 interface:

PROC ACCESS
    ACCDESC=*libref.access-descriptor*
    ALIB=*libref*
    DBMS=S2K
    FUNCTION=C | U | ED
    OUT=*libref.member*
    VIEWDESC=*libref.view-descriptor*;
  CREATE *libref.member-name.type*;
  ASSIGN<=>YES | NO;
  BYKEY *variable-identifier-1*<=>YES | NO <. . . *variable-identifier-n*<=>YES | NO>;
  DATABASE < = > *database-name*
    S2KPW<=>*password* <MODE<=>SINGLE | MULTI>;
  DROP *variable-identifier-1* <. . . *variable-identifier-n*>;
  FORMAT *variable-identifier-1*<=>*SAS-format-name-1*
    <. . . *variable-identifier-n*<=>*SAS-format-name-n*>;
  INFORMAT *variable-identifier-1*<=>*SAS-informat-name-1*
    <. . . *variable-identifier-n*<=>*SAS-informat-name-n*>;
  LENGTH *variable-identifier-1*<=>*item-width-1*
    <. . . *variable-identifier-n*<=>*item-width-n*>;
  LIST <ALL | VIEW | *variable-identifier*>;
  QUIT;
  RENAME *variable-identifier-1*<=>*SAS-variable-name-1*
    <. . . *variable-identifier-n*<=>*SAS-variable-name-n*>;
  RESET ALL | *variable-identifier-1* <. . . *variable-identifier-n*>;
  SELECT ALL | *variable-identifier-1* <. . . *variable-identifier-n*>;
  SUBSET *selection-criteria*;
  S2KPW<=>*password* <MODE<=>MULTI | SINGLE>;
  UNIQUE<=>YES | NO;

For interactive line mode, enter these statements at the ? prompt. For noninteractive and batch jobs, surround your SAS statements with any appropriate operating system-specific statements and submit the job for processing.

PROC ACCESS Statement Options

The following options can be used with the PROC ACCESS statement. The options you use depend on your goal (creating an access descriptor, editing a view descriptor, and so on) and on the method of processing you choose. For easier reference, all the PROC ACCESS options are described in this section, including those that have not changed in Release 6.07.

Most of the options can only be used with a particular method of operation, which is highlighted in boldface. This section distinquishes between **display manager mode** and the **other modes** (that is, interactive line, noninteractive, or batch mode). See "Running the SAS System" in "Using This Book" for more information on these SAS methods of operation.

ACCDESC=*libref.access-descriptor*   (**all modes**)
ACCESS=
AD=
   identifies an access descriptor.
      Other modes: You use this option to create view descriptors from an existing access descriptor.
      If the access descriptor has been assigned a SAS password, you may need to specify the password in the ACCDESC= option in order to create a view descriptor based on the access descriptor. Whether you specify the password depends on the level of protection that was assigned to the access descriptor. For example, the following access descriptor, SASUSER.SALARIES, has a password (MONEY) assigned to it with the ALTER level of protection. Therefore, the password must be specified using the ALTER= SAS data set option before you are allowed to create view descriptors based on SASUSER.SALARIES.

```
proc access dbms=s2k accdesc=sasuser.salaries(alter=money);
```

See "Specifying SAS System Passwords for SAS/ACCESS Descriptors" later in this chapter for more information on assigning and using passwords.
      If you create the access descriptor and the view descriptor in the same execution of PROC ACCESS, omit the ACCDESC= option because you specify the access descriptor's name in the CREATE statement.
      Display manager mode: You can use the ACCDESC= option (in combination with the FUNCTION= option) to create an access descriptor and bypass the ACCESS window. See the Release 6.06 documentation for your SAS/ACCESS interface for more information and examples.
      AD= and ACCESS= are aliases for this option.

ALIB=*libref*   (**display manager mode only**)
   specifies the SAS data library that contains the access descriptor for the view descriptor you want to edit. You use the ALIB= option in conjunction with the VIEWDESC= option.
      If you omit this option, the SAS System searches all SAS data libraries allocated to your session until it finds an access descriptor with the correct name. Using the ALIB= option may save you time if you have several SAS data libraries allocated to your SAS session. The ALIB= option also prevents you from using the wrong access descriptor if you have two access descriptors with the same name but in different libraries.

DBMS=S2K   (**other modes only**)
   specifies you want to invoke the SAS/ACCESS interface to SYSTEM 2000 software. This option is required when creating a descriptor but not when extracting DBMS data.

FUNCTION=C | U | ED   **(display manager mode only)**
FUNC=
> specifies whether you want to create a new access descriptor or update an existing access descriptor. You specify the FUNCTION= option after the ACCDESC= option.
>
> You specify the C value to create an access descriptor or the U or E value to update an existing access descriptor. You can edit an access descriptor only using windows.
>
> In interactive line, noninteractive, and batch modes, the CREATE statement supercedes the FUNCTION=C option. If you specify FUNCTION=C, it is ignored in these modes.

OUT=*libref.member*   **(other modes only)**
> identifies the SAS data file that stores extracted DBMS data.

VIEWDESC=*libref.view-descriptor*   **(all modes)**
VIEW=
VD=
> identifies a view descriptor.
>
> **Display manager mode:** You use this option to specify the view descriptor to be edited. You can edit a view descriptor only in this mode.
>
> **Other modes:** You use the VIEWDESC= option to extract DBMS data and to place them in a SAS data file. When extracting DBMS data, you must specify the OUT= option after the VIEWDESC= option.

See "Examples" later in this chapter for examples of using options in procedure statements.

Procedure Statements

The procedure statements for PROC ACCESS enable you to create access and view descriptors in interactive line mode, noninteractive mode, and batch mode. (See "Running the SAS System" in "Using This Book" for more information on these SAS methods of operation. The statements you use depend on your purpose, such as creating only an access descriptor, creating only a view descriptor, or creating both types of descriptors. The statements and options that identify the database, password, and mode (DATABASE=, S2KPW=, and MODE=) must be submitted after the CREATE statement and before you begin to define access or view descriptors based on that information, including the ASSIGN or UNIQUE statement.

The following procedure statements are available with PROC ACCESS for SYSTEM 2000 software:

CREATE *libref.member-name.type*;
> identifies an access descriptor or view descriptor you want to create. The CREATE statement is required.
>
> To create the descriptor, use a three-level name. The first level is the libref of the SAS data library where you want the descriptor stored. You can store the descriptor in a temporary (WORK) or permanent SAS data library. The second level is the access descriptor's name (that is, the member name). The third level is the type of SAS file: ACCESS for access descriptors and VIEW for view descriptors.

When you submit a CREATE statement for processing, the SAS/ACCESS interface checks the statement for errors. The descriptor is not actually written until the next CREATE or RUN statement is processed. If the SAS/ACCESS interface does find errors, error messages are written to the SAS log and processing is terminated. After you correct the error, resubmit the statements for processing.

Creating access descriptors
To create an access descriptor, the CREATE statement must follow the PROC ACCESS statement. It is specified before any of the other statements. For example, you could specify the following:

```
proc access dbms=s2k;
   create mylib.employe.access;
      database-identifier statement(s);
      optional editing statement(s);
run;
```

You can create one or more view descriptors based on this access descriptor within the same execution of the procedure, as described later in this section.

Creating view descriptors
You also use the CREATE statement to create a view descriptor. You can create a view descriptor in the same execution or in a separate execution of the ACCESS procedure.

To create a view descriptor in the same execution of PROC ACCESS, add the CREATE statement after the procedure statements that create the access descriptor on which this view descriptor is based. For example, you could specify the following:

```
proc access dbms=s2k;
   create mylib.employe.access;
      database-identifier statement(s);
      optional editing statement(s);

   create vlib.emppos.view;
      select variable-list;
      optional editing statement(s);
run;
```

If you create a view based on an existing access descriptor (that is, one created in a previous execution of the ACCESS procedure), specify the access descriptor's name in the ACCDESC= option in the PROC ACCESS statement and follow it with a CREATE statement. Place any editing and view descriptor-specific statements, such as SELECT and SUBSET, after the view descriptor's CREATE statement. For example, you could specify the following:

```
proc access dbms=s2k accdesc=mylib.employe;
   create vlib.emppos.view;
      select variable-list;
      optional editing statement(s);
      subset where-expression;
```

(CREATE libref.member-name.type; continued)

```
              create vlib.empskil.view;
                 select variable-list;
                 optional editing statement(s);
         run;
```

When you specify the ACCDESC= option in the PROC ACCESS statement, you can use CREATE statements only to create view descriptors. You can issue multiple CREATE statements to create views based on the specified access descriptor.

The database-identifier and DROP statements cannot be specified when creating a view descriptor in interactive line, noninteractive, or batch mode.

ASSIGN | AN<=>YES | NO | Y | N;
generates SAS variable names based on the first eight, non-blank characters of the item names. It also generates SAS variable attributes based on the items' data types. The ASSIGN statement is specified only when creating an access descriptor.

The default value NO (or N) permits you to modify SAS variable attributes when you create the access descriptor and when you create view descriptors based on this access descriptor. You use the RENAME statement to change the variable names during a descriptor's creation.

Specifying a YES (or Y) value for this statement also generates SAS variable names, but these names can only be changed in the access descriptor. The names saved in the access descriptor are always used in view descriptors created from this access descriptor. This statement prevents you from changing the names when you create a view descriptor.

If you specify a YES value for this statement, the SAS System automatically resolves any duplicate variable names. However, with a YES value, you cannot specify the BYKEY, FORMAT, INFORMAT, LENGTH, RENAME, and UNIQUE statements when creating view descriptors based on this access descriptor.

When the interface encounters the next CREATE statement to create an access descriptor, the ASSIGN statement is reset to the default NO value.

AN is the alias for the ASSIGN statement.

BYKEY *variable-identifier-1*<=>YES | NO
  <. . . *variable-identifier-n*<=>YES | NO>;
designates one or more items as BY keys. If the ASSIGN statement is specified with a YES (or Y) value, the BYKEY statement cannot be used to change BY keys in view descriptors created from that access descriptor. The default value is NO (or N). The BYKEY statement only applies to data items. Using the equal sign (=) is optional.

The *variable-identifier* argument can be one of the following:

□ current SAS name for the item
   Note: Any name on the lefthand side of the equal sign must be a SAS name, not a SYSTEM 2000 name. If the ASSIGN statement is omitted, you must use the item number or component number (C-number) on the lefthand side of the equal sign.

□ positional equivalent, which is the number that represents the item, as given by the LIST statement

□ SYSTEM 2000 C-number of the database item.

For example, if you want to make the third item a BY key, issue the following statement:

```
bykey 3=y;
```

This statement is used when creating or editing both access descriptors and view descriptors. If you use a BYKEY statement for a view descriptor, the item is automatically selected for the view.

DATABASE < = > *database-name* S2KPW<=>*password*
  <MODE<=>*access-mode*>;
  specifies the name of the SYSTEM 2000 database you want to use. The DATABASE statement should immediately follow the CREATE statement for the access descriptor being created. If the database name contains blanks or special characters, enclose the name in single or double quotes. The equal sign (=) is optional when specifying the database name. DB, DBN, and S2KDB are aliases for the DATABASE statement.
  The DATABASE statement takes two arguments, as follows:

S2KPW<=>*password*
  is the SYSTEM 2000 password for the database you want to use. The equal sign (=) is optional when specifying the password. This argument is required.

MODE<=>SINGLE | MULTI
  specifies your mode of accessing SYSTEM 2000 software. SINGLE means the database is in a single-user environment (that is, a database in your SAS program environment). MULTI means the database files are in the Multi-User environment. The equal sign (=) is optional when specifying the access mode. The default value is MULTI. The SINGLE value can be abbreviated as SU or S. The MULTI value can be abbreviated as MU or M. MD, S2KMD, and S2KMODE are aliases for the MODE argument. The MODE argument is optional.
  The DATABASE statement is only used when creating access descriptors. Use the S2KPW= statement if you want to specify a password or access mode for view descriptors.

DROP *variable-identifier-1* <. . . *variable-identifier-n*>;
  drops the specified variable from the access descriptor so that the variable is no longer available for selection when creating a view descriptor. The specified variable in the database remains unaffected by this statement. If you drop a record, every item in the record is dropped. The DROP statement is specified only when creating an access descriptor in interactive line, noninteractive, or batch mode. This statement is optional.
  The *variable-identifier* argument can be one of the following:

□ current SAS name for the item

□ positional equivalent, which is the number that represents the item, as given by the LIST statement

□ SYSTEM 2000 C-number of the database item.

(DROP variable-identifier-1 continued)

For example, if you want to drop the third and fifth items, submit the following statement:

```
drop 3 5;
```

If you are creating an access descriptor and want to mark an item as display that was previously marked as non-display with the DROP statement, use the RESET statement for that item. Note, however, that this will also reset the various attributes of that item to their default values (such as name, format, and so on).

FORMAT *variable-identifier-1*<=>*SAS-format-name-1*
<. . . *variable-identifier-n*<=>*SAS-format-name-n*>;
changes a SAS variable format from its default format; the default format is based on the database item's data type. You can enter formats for as many items as necessary using one FORMAT statement. The FORMAT statement can be used when creating an access descriptor or a view descriptor. This statement is optional.

Note that the equal sign (=) is optional between arguments. You cannot specify the FORMAT statement for a record.

The *variable-identifier* argument can be one of the following:

□   current SAS variable name for the item
    Note: Any name on the lefthand side of the equal sign must be a SAS name, not a SYSTEM 2000 name. If the ASSIGN statement is omitted, you must use the item number or component number (C-number) on the lefthand side of the equal sign.

□   positional equivalent, which is the number that represents the item, as given by the LIST statement

□   SYSTEM 2000 C-number of the database item.

For example, if you want to associate the DATE9. format with the fifth item in the access descriptor, issue the following statement:

```
format 5 date9.;
```

The FORMAT statement is used when creating either an access descriptor or a view descriptor. You can only use the FORMAT statement with a view descriptor if the ASSIGN statement used when creating the access descriptor was specified with the NO value. When used for a view descriptor, the FORMAT statement automatically selects the reformatted item. That is, if you change the format associated with an item, you do not have to issue a SELECT statement for that item.

FMT is an alias for the FORMAT statement.

INFORMAT *variable-identifier-1*<=>*SAS-informat-name-1*
<. . . *variable-identifier-n*<=>*SAS-informat-name-n*>;
changes a SAS variable informat from its default informat; the default informat is based on the database item's data type. You can enter as many informats as necessary using one INFORMAT statement. The INFORMAT

statement can be used when creating an access descriptor or a view descriptor. This statement is optional.

Note that the equal sign (=) is optional. You cannot specify the INFORMAT statement for a record.

The *variable-identifier* argument can be one of the following:

☐ current SAS variable name for the item
   Note: Any name on the lefthand side of the equal sign must be a SAS name, not a SYSTEM 2000 name. If the ASSIGN statement is omitted, you must use the item number or component number (C-number) on the lefthand side of the equal sign.

☐ positional equivalent, which is the number that represents the item, as given by the LIST statement

☐ SYSTEM 2000 C-number of the database item.

For example, if you want to associate the DATE7. informat with the second item in the access descriptor, issue the following statement:

```
informat 2 DATE7.;
```

The INFORMAT statement is used when creating either an access descriptor or a view descriptor. You can only use the INFORMAT statement with a view descriptor if the ASSIGN statement is specified with the NO value. When used for a view descriptor, the INFORMAT statement automatically selects the reformatted item. That is, if you change the informat associated with an item, you do not have to issue a SELECT statement for that item.

INF is an alias for the INFORMAT statement.

LENGTH *variable-identifier-1*<=>*item-width-1*
   <. . . *variable-identifier-n*<=>*item-width-n*>;
changes the item width in characters from the default width; the default item width is based on the database item's picture specification. This statement enables the SAS System to deal with S2K CHARACTER/TEXT items that overflow their widths (the SAS System does not permit variable-length character variables). The *item-width* argument can be no greater than 200. The LENGTH statement can be used when creating an access descriptor or a view descriptor in interactive line, noninteractive, or batch mode. This statement is optional.

Note that the equal sign (=) is optional. The LENGTH statement only applies to data items; you cannot specify a length for a record.

The *variable-identifier* argument can be one of the following:

☐ current SAS name for the item
   Note: Any name on the lefthand side of the equal sign must be a SAS name, not a SYSTEM 2000 name. If the ASSIGN statement is omitted, you must use the item number or component number (C-number) on the lefthand side of the equal sign.

☐ positional equivalent, which is the number that represents the item, as given by the LIST statement

☐ SYSTEM 2000 C-number of the database item.

(LENGTH variable-identifier-1 continued)

The LENGTH statement is used when creating an access descriptor or a view descriptor. You can only use the LENGTH statement with a view descriptor if the ASSIGN statement is specified with the NO value. When used for a view descriptor, the LENGTH statement automatically selects the reformatted item. That is, if you change the length associated with an item, you do not have to issue a SELECT statement for that item.

LEN and S2KLEN are aliases for the LENGTH statement.

LIST <ALL | VIEW | *variable-identifier*>;

lists all or selected items in the descriptor and attributes of items, including their positional equivalents, SYSTEM 2000 component numbers, default SAS variable names based on the first eight, non-blank characters of the SYSTEM 2000 item names, and the default SAS formats based on the SYSTEM 2000 data types.

Note: The SYSTEM 2000 item names are not listed in the log because of their possible 40 or more character length.

The LIST statement can be used when creating an access descriptor or a view descriptor in interactive line, noninteractive, or batch mode. In noninteractive and batch modes, the LIST information is written to your SAS log. This statement is optional.

The LIST statement can take one or more of the following arguments:

ALL
lists all items and item attributes available in the access descriptor for selection. If an item has been dropped when creating an access descriptor, *NON-DISPLAY* is shown next to the item's description. When creating a view descriptor, items selected for the view are shown with *SELECTED* next to the item's description.

If you do not specify an argument, the default is ALL.

VIEW
lists all items and item attributes in the access descriptor selected for the view descriptor and any subsetting or ordering criteria. The VIEW argument is only valid when creating a view descriptor.

variable-identifier
the current SAS name, the positional equivalent (which is the number that represents the item, as given by the LIST statement), or the SYSTEM 2000 C-number of the database item.

If you specify a record in a LIST statement, all the data items in that record are listed.

For example, if you want to list information about the fifth item in the database, issue the following statement:

```
list 5;
```

You can use one or more of these options in a LIST statement, in any order. Here is an example:

```
list all view;
```

This statement lists all the items in the database, followed by the items selected for the view descriptor.

QUIT | EXIT;

terminates the ACCESS procedure without any further descriptor creation. The QUIT statement can be used when creating a descriptor in interactive line, noninteractive, or batch mode. This statement is optional. EXIT is the alias for the QUIT statement.

RENAME *variable-identifier-1*<=>*SAS-variable-name-1*
  <. . . *variable-identifier-n*<=>*SAS-variable-name-n*;

enters or modifies the SAS variable name associated with a database item. The RENAME statement can be used when creating an access descriptor or a view descriptor. This statement is optional.

Two factors affect the use of the RENAME statement: whether you specify the ASSIGN statement when creating an access descriptor and the kind of descriptor you are creating.

□ If you omit the ASSIGN statement or specify it with a NO value, the renamed SAS variable names you specify in the access descriptor are retained throughout an ACCESS procedure execution. If you rename the CUSTOMER item to CUSTNUM when creating an access descriptor, that item continues to be named CUSTNUM when you select it in a view descriptor based on the access descriptor unless a RESET statement or another RENAME statement is specified.

When creating a view descriptor based on this access descriptor, you can specify the RESET statement or another RENAME statement to rename the variable again, but the new name applies only in that view. When creating other view descriptors, the SAS variable names and attributes will be derived from the access descriptor.

□ If you specify the YES value in the ASSIGN statement, you can only use the RENAME statement to change SAS variable names while creating an access descriptor. As described earlier in the ASSIGN statement, SAS variable names and attributes saved in the access descriptor are always used when creating view descriptors based on it. If ASSIGN=Y, you can assign new SAS names to the default SAS names.

The *variable-identifier* argument can be one of the following:

□ current SAS variable name for the item
  Note: Any name on the lefthand side of the equal sign must be a SAS name, not a SYSTEM 2000 name. If the ASSIGN statement is omitted, you must use an item number or component number (C-number) on the lefthand side of the equal sign.

□ positional equivalent from the LIST statement, which is the number that represents the item's place in the descriptor

□ SYSTEM 2000 C-number of the database item.

For example, if you want to modify the SAS variable names associated with the fourth and fifth items in a descriptor, issue the following statement:

(RENAME variable-identifier-1 continued)

```
rename 4=hire birthday=birth;
```

The equal sign (=) is optional.

When creating a view descriptor, the RENAME statement automatically selects the renamed item for the view. That is, if you rename the SAS variable associated with a database item, you do not have to issue a SELECT statement for that item.

RESET ALL | *variable-identifier-1* <. . . *variable-identifier-n*>;
resets all or the specified items to their default values. The RESET statement can be used when creating an access descriptor or a view descriptor in interactive line, noninteractive, or batch mode. However, this statement has different effects on access and view descriptors, as described in the following information. The RESET statement is optional.

Access descriptors

When creating an access descriptor, the default setting for a SAS variable name is a blank, unless you enter SAS variable names using the RENAME statement or include the ASSIGN=YES statement. If you entered or modified any SAS variable name, the name is reset to the default name generated by the ACCESS procedure (that is, the first eight characters of the variable name).

The item's variable attributes are reset to the default attributes, which are determined from the item's database type and picture specification. If the item was dropped using the DROP statement, it is now available and can be selected in view descriptors based on this access descriptor.

View descriptors

When creating a view descriptor, the RESET statement clears any items included in the SELECT statement (that is, it unselects the items).

When creating the view descriptor, if you reset SAS variable names and variable attributes and then select them later within the same procedure execution, the SAS variable names and attributes are reset to the default values generated from the item names and data types. This applies only if you have omitted the ASSIGN statement or specified the NO value in it when you created the access descriptor on which the view descriptor is based. If you specified the ASSIGN=YES statement when you created the access descriptor, the view descriptor's SAS variable names and attributes are unaffected by the RESET statement.

The RESET statement can take one or more of the following arguments:

ALL
resets all the database items defined in the access descriptor to their default name and attribute settings. When creating a view descriptor, the ALL argument resets all the items that have been selected, so that no items are selected for the view; you can then use the SELECT statement to select new items. See the SELECT statement later in this chapter for more information.

variable-identifier   can be the current SAS name, the positional equivalent (which is the number that represents the item as given by the LIST statement), or the SYSTEM 2000 component number of the database item.

    Note: Any name on the lefthand side of the equal sign must be a SAS name, not a SYSTEM 2000 name. If the ASSIGN statement is omitted, you must use the item number or component number (C-number) on the lefthand side of the equal sign.

    For example, if you want to reset the SAS variable name and attribute associated with the third item, issue the following statement:

```
reset 3;
```

If you specify a name in the RESET statement, you must specify a SAS name, not a SYSTEM 2000 name. You can reset as many items as you want using one RESET statement or the ALL option to reset all the items.

    When creating an access descriptor, the item indicated by the *variable-identifier* argument is reset to its default name and attribute settings. When creating a view descriptor, the specified item is no longer selected for the view.

SELECT ALL | *variable-identifier-1* <. . . *variable-identifier-n*>;

selects the database items in the access descriptor to be included in the view descriptor.

    The SELECT statement can take one or more of the following arguments:

ALL   includes in the view descriptor all the items defined in the access descriptor that were not dropped.

variable-identifier   can be the current SAS name, the positional equivalent (which is the number that represents the item as given by the LIST statement), or the SYSTEM 2000 component number of the database item.

    Note: Any name on the lefthand side of the equal sign must be a SAS name, not a SYSTEM 2000 name. If the ASSIGN statement is omitted, you must use the item number or component number (C-number) on the lefthand side of the equal sign.

    For example, if you want to select the first three items, issue the following statement:

```
select 1 2 3;
```

You can select as many items as you want using one SELECT statement.

    SELECT statements are cumulative within the same view creation. That is, if you submit the following two SELECT statements, items 1, 5, and 6 are selected (not just items 5 and 6):

(SELECT ALL continued)

```
select 1;
select 5 6;
```

To clear all your current selections when creating a view descriptor, you can use the RESET ALL statement; you can then use another SELECT statement to select new items.

Selecting a record selects all items within the record.

SUBSET *selection-criteria*;

specifies the selection criteria when creating a view descriptor. The SUBSET statement is optional, but omitting it causes the view to retrieve all the data in the database. For example, you can issue the following statement:

```
subset "where amount<1010";
```

If you have multiple selection criteria, enter them all in one SUBSET statement, as in the following example:

```
subset "where amount<1010"
       "ob amount";
```

The quoted strings are concatenated and passed to SYSTEM 2000 software for processing.

For more information on selection and ordering criteria for the SAS/ACCESS interface to SYSTEM 2000 data management software, refer to your Release 6.06 SAS/ACCESS documentation.

To clear the selection criteria, issue a SUBSET statement without an argument, as follows:

```
subset;
```

S2KPW<=>*password* <MODE<=>MULTI | SINGLE>;

specifies the SYSTEM 2000 password and optional mode for creating view descriptors only. (You use the DATABASE statement to assign a password to an access descriptor.)

If you use an S2KPW statement when creating or editing a view descriptor, the password you specify in the S2KPW statement is stored in encrypted form with the view. The equal sign (=) is optional when specifying the password.

The S2KPW statement takes one optional argument, as follows:

MODE<=>SINGLE | MULTI

specifies your mode of accessing SYSTEM 2000 software. SINGLE means the database is in a single-user environment (that is, a database in your SAS program environment). MULTI means the database files are in the Multi-User environment. The equal sign (=) is optional when specifying the access mode. The default value is MULTI. The SINGLE value can be abbreviated as SU or S. The MULTI value can be abbreviated as MU or M. MD, S2KMD, and S2KMODE are aliases for the MODE argument. If you specify the mode when creating or editing a view descriptor, the mode is stored with the view.

UNIQUE<=>YES | NO | Y | N;
UN<=>YES | NO | Y | N;

specifies whether the SAS/ACCESS interface should generate unique SAS variable names for items for which SAS variable names or variable attributes have not been entered. The UNIQUE statement is optional and is used only when creating view descriptors in interactive line, noninteractive, or batch mode.

Use of the UNIQUE statement is affected by whether you specified the ASSIGN statement when creating the access descriptor on which this view is based.

❑ If you specified the ASSIGN statement with a YES value, you cannot specify the UNIQUE statement when creating a view. The YES value causes the SAS System to generate unique names, so the UNIQUE statement is not necessary.

❑ If you omitted the ASSIGN statement or specified it with a NO value, you must resolve any duplicate SAS variable names in the view descriptor. You can use the UNIQUE statement to automatically generate unique names, or you can use the RENAME statement to resolve these duplicate names yourself. See the RENAME statement earlier in this chapter for information on it.

If duplicate SAS variable names exist in the access descriptor on which you are creating a view descriptor, you can specify the UNIQUE statement to resolve the duplication. You specify the YES (or Y) value to have the SAS/ACCESS interface append numbers to any duplicate SAS variable names, thus making each variable name unique.

If you specify a NO (or N) value for the UNIQUE statement, the SAS/ACCESS interface continues to allow duplicate SAS variable names to exist. You must resolve these duplicate names before saving (and thereby creating) the view descriptor.

If you are running your SAS/ACCESS job in noninteractive or batch mode, it is recommended that you use the UNIQUE statement. If you do not and the SAS System encounters duplicate SAS variable names in a view descriptor, your job will fail.

The equal sign (=) is optional in the UNIQUE statement. UN is the alias for this statement.

Examples

This section presents some examples of creating access descriptors and view descriptors using the PROC ACCESS options and statements described previously.

You can submit these examples in a SAS program from the PROGRAM EDITOR window, one line at a time in interactive line mode, or surround the program with the appropriate operating system statements and submit the job in batch mode.

Creating Access and View Descriptors in One PROC Step

Perhaps the most common way to use the ACCESS procedure statements, especially in batch mode, is to create an access descriptor and one or more view descriptors based on this access descriptor in a single PROC ACCESS execution. The following example shows how to do this. First, an access descriptor is created (MYLIB.EMPLOYE). Then two view descriptors are created, named VLIB.EMPPOS and VLIB.EMPSKIL. Each statement is then explained in the order it appears in the example program.

```
proc access dbms=s2k;
    create mylib.employe.access;
        database=employee s2kpw=mine mode=multi;
        assign=yes;
        drop c110 c120;
        rename forename=firstnam office_e=phone
               yearsofe=years degree_c=degree;
        length firstnam=10 c101=16;
        list all;

    create vlib.emppos.view;
        select lastname firstnam positio1 departme manager;
        subset "where sex=female
               order by lastname";
        list all;

    create vlib.empskil.view;
        select c2 c3 c201 c203;
        subset "ob skilltyp";
        s2kpw=mine mode=multi;
        list view;
    run;
```

Here is an explanation of the statements in this example:

proc access dbms=s2k;
invokes the ACCESS procedure for the SAS/ACCESS interface to SYSTEM 2000 software.

create mylib.employe.access;
identifies the access descriptor, MYLIB.EMPLOYE, that you want to create. The MYLIB libref must be associated with the SAS data library before you can specify it in this statement.

database=employee s2kpw=mine mode=multi;
indicates the access descriptor is for the EMPLOYEE database, specifies the password, MINE, required to access the database definition, and indicates the database is in the Multi-User environment.

assign=yes;
generates unique SAS variable names based on the first eight non-blank characters of the item names. Variable names and attributes can be changed

in this access descriptor but not in any view descriptors created from this access descriptor.

`drop c110 c120;`
> marks the records associated with C-numbers C110 and C120 as non-display. Because these two C-numbers indicate records, all the items in each record are marked as non-display. Therefore, all the items in the two records associated with these numbers do not appear in any view descriptor created from this access descriptor.

`rename forename=firstnam office_e=phone`
`    yearsofe=years degree_c=degree;`
> renames the default SAS variable names associated with the FORENAME, OFFICE_E, YEARSOFE, and DEGREE_C SAS names. When the ASSIGN statement is included, you specify the default SAS variable names on the left side of the equal sign (=). Because the ASSIGN=YES statement is specified, any view descriptors created from this access descriptor automatically use the new SAS variable names.

`length firstnam=10 c101=16;`
> changes the field width for the item associated with FIRSTNAM to 10 characters and the field width for the item associated with C-number C101 (the POSITIO1 SAS name) to 16 characters.

`list all;`
> lists the access descriptor's item identifier numbers, C-numbers, SAS variable names, SAS formats, SAS informats, and SAS variable lengths. The list includes any associated BY key information. In noninteractive and batch modes, the list is written to the SAS log. Any items that have been dropped from display (using the DROP statement) have *NON-DISPLAY* next to them.

`create vlib.emppos.view;`
> writes the access descriptor to the library associated with MYLIB and identifies the view descriptor, VLIB.EMPPOS, that you want to create. The VLIB libref must be associated with a SAS data library before you can specify it in this statement.

`select lastname firstnam positio1 departme manager;`
> selects the items associated with the LASTNAME, FIRSTNAM, POSITIO1, DEPARTME, and MANAGER SAS names for inclusion in the view descriptor. The SELECT statement is required to create the view unless a RENAME, FORMAT, INFORMAT, LENGTH, or BYKEY statement is specified.

`subset "where sex=female`
`    order by lastname";`
> specifies you want the view descriptor to include only observations for female employees. The names in the output are ordered by the last names. Using the word WHERE is optional. Use the SAS/ACCESS interface to SYSTEM 2000 syntax in the SUBSET statement.

`list all;`
> lists all the available item identifier numbers, C-numbers, SAS variable names, SAS formats, SAS informats, and SAS variable lengths on which the view descriptor is based; items that have been dropped from the display have *NON-DISPLAY* next to them. Any associated BY key information is also listed. Selection criteria specified in the view descriptor are listed. Items that

(list all; continued)

have been selected for the view have *SELECTED* next to them. In noninteractive and batch modes, the list is written to the SAS log.

`create vlib.empskil.view;`
writes the first view descriptor to the library associated with VLIB and identifies the next view descriptor, VLIB.EMPSKIL, that you want to create.

`select c2 c3 c201 c203;`
selects the four items associated with C-numbers C2, C3, C201 and C203 for inclusion in the view descriptor. The SELECT statement is required to create the view unless a RENAME, FORMAT, INFORMAT, LENGTH, or BYKEY statement is specified.

`subset "ob skilltyp";`
specifies you want the observations to be sorted by skill type. Use the SAS/ACCESS interface to SYSTEM 2000 syntax in the SUBSET statement.

`s2kpw=mine mode=multi;`
specifies the password required to access the data and indicates the database is in the Multi-User environment. This information is stored in the view descriptor.

`list view;`
lists the item identifier numbers, the C-numbers, the SAS variable names, the SAS formats, the SAS informats, and the SAS variable lengths that have been selected for the view descriptor. Any associated BY key information is also listed. Selection criteria specified in the view descriptor are listed. In noninteractive and batch modes, the list is written to the SAS log.

`run;`
writes the last view descriptor when the RUN statement is processed.

Creating Access Descriptors

You use the CREATE statement in the ACCESS procedure to create access descriptors. You can either create a single access descriptor or several access descriptors in the same procedure execution.

Creating a Single Access Descriptor

The following example creates a single access descriptor, named MYLIB.BNKINFO, for a SYSTEM 2000 database. Each statement is then explained in the order it appears in the example program.

```
proc access dbms=s2k;
   create mylib.bnkinfo.access;
      database=banking s2kpw=mine mode=single;
      assign=yes;
      rename accountn=acct_num c102=acct_typ
             9=trdate;
      format c104=12.4;
```

```
      listall;
  run;
```

Here is an explanation of the statements in this example:

`proc access dbms=s2k;`
> invokes the ACCESS procedure for the SAS/ACCESS interface for SYSTEM 2000 software.

`create mylib.bnkinfo.access;`
> identifies the access descriptor, MYLIB.BNKINFO, that you want to create. The MYLIB libref must be associated with a SAS data library before you can specify it in this statement.

`database=banking s2kpw=mine mode=single;`
> indicates the access descriptor is for the BANKING database, specifies the password, MINE, required to access the banking database definition, and indicates the database is in the single-user environment.

`assign=yes;`
> generates SAS variable names based on the first eight characters of the item names. You cannot change SAS names and attributes in any views created from this descriptor.

`rename accountn=acct_num c102=acct_typ`
`   9=trdate;`
> renames the SAS variables associated with the ACCOUNTN variable (the current SAS name), C-number C102, and item identifier number 9.

`format c104=12.4;`
> assigns the 12.4 format to the TRANSAMT variable associated with C-number C104. Using an equal sign is optional.

`list all;`
> lists the access descriptor's item identifier numbers, C-numbers , SAS variable names, SAS formats, SAS informats, and SAS variable lengths. Any associated BY key information is also listed. In noninteractive or batch mode, the list is written to the SAS log. Any items dropped from display have *NON-DISPLAY* next to them.

`run;`
> writes the access descriptor when the RUN statement is processed.

Creating Several Access Descriptors

It is possible to create several access descriptors in one execution of the ACCESS procedure. The following program creates two access descriptors, named MYLIB.POSITN and MYLIB.EDUC, from two separate SYSTEM 2000 databases. Each statement is then explained in the order it appears in the example program.

```
proc access dbms=s2k;
   create mylib.positn.access;
      database=employee s2kpw=job mode=multi;
      drop c200 c300 c400;
      rename c101=title c102=dept
             c104=postype c124=gros_pay
             c114=c_deduct c125=f_deduct;
```

```
        format c111=dollar12.2 c124=dollar12.2
               c126=dollar12.2 c114=dollar12.2
               c125=dollar12.2;
        list all;
   create mylib.educ.access;
      database=personnel s2kpw=edu mode=multi;
      drop c17;
      length c164 30;
      format c163=date9.;
run;
```

Here is an explanation of the statements in this example:

`proc access dbms=s2k;`
   invokes the ACCESS procedure for the SAS/ACCESS interface to SYSTEM 2000 software.

`create mylib.positn.access;`
   identifies the access descriptor, MYLIB.POSITN, that you want to create. The MYLIB libref must be associated with a SAS data library before you can specify it in this statement.

`database=employee s2kpw=job mode=multi;`
   indicates the access descriptor is for the EMPLOYEE database, specifies the password, JOB, required to access the employee database definition, and indicates the database is in the Multi-User environment.

`drop c200 c300 c400;`
   marks the records associated with C-numbers C200, C300, and C400 as non-display. Because these three C-numbers indicate records, all the items in each record are marked as non-display. Therefore, all the items in the three records associated with these numbers do not appear in any view descriptor created from this access descriptor.

`rename c101=title c102=dept`
`    c104=postype c124=gros_pay`
`    c114=c_deduct c125=f_deduct;`
   renames the SAS variables associated with C-numbers C101, C102, C104, C114, C124, and C125. If the ASSIGN statement is omitted, you must use the item numbers or C-numbers on the lefthand side of the equal sign because SAS names have not been created.

`format c111=dollar12.2 c124=dollar12.2`
`c126=dollar12.2 c114=dollar12.2   c125=dollar12.2;`
   assigns the SAS format DOLLAR12.2 to the SAS variables associated with C-numbers C111, C114, C124, C125, and C126. If the ASSIGN statement is omitted, you must use the item numbers or C-numbers on the lefthand side of the equal sign because SAS names have not been created.

`list all;`
   lists the access descriptor's item identifiers, SAS variable names, SAS formats, SAS informats, and SAS variable lengths. Any associated BY key information is also listed. In noninteractive and batch modes, the list is written to the SAS log. Any items dropped from display (using the DROP statement) have *NON-DISPLAY* next to them.

```
create mylib.educ.access;
```
writes the first access descriptor to the library associated with MYLIB and identifies another access descriptor (MYLIB.EDUC) that you want to create.

```
database=personnel s2kpw=edu mode=multi;
```
identifies a new database, PERSONNEL, specifies the EDU password required to access the database definition, and indicates the database is in the Multi-User environment.

```
drop c17;
```
marks the record associated with C-number C17 as non-display. Because this C-number indicates a record, all the items in the record are marked as non-display. Therefore, all the items in the record associated with C-number C17 do not appear in any view descriptor created from this access descriptor.

```
length c164 30;
```
changes the field width for the item associated with C-number C164 to 30 characters.

```
format c163=date9.;
```
assigns the SAS format DATE9. to the SAS variable associated with C-number C163.

```
run;
```
writes the last access descriptor when the RUN statement is processed.

Creating View Descriptors

To use the ACCESS procedure to create view descriptors, invoke the procedure with the ACCDESC= option. You can either create a single view descriptor or create several in the same procedure execution.

Creating a Single View Descriptor

You can use the ACCESS procedure to create a view descriptors from an existing access descriptor, as in the following example. This example creates a view descriptor named VLIB.SALARY from an access descriptor named MYLIB.POSITN. Each statement is then explained in the order it appears in the example program.

```
proc access dbms=s2k accdesc=mylib.positn;
   create vlib.salary.view;
      s2kpw=mine mode=single;
      reset all;
      unique=yes;
      select lastname forename c5 c6 c7 c8 c101 c120;
      subset "departme=corporation
              ob gross pay";
      list view;
run;
```

Here is an explanation of the statements in this example:

```
proc access dbms=s2k accdesc=mylib.positn;
```
invokes the ACCESS procedure for the SAS/ACCESS interface to SYSTEM 2000 software and specifies that the view descriptors will be created based on the access descriptor MYLIB.POSITN. The MYLIB libref must be associated with a SAS data library before you can specify it in the ACCDESC= option.

```
create vlib.salary.view;
```
identifies the view descriptor, VLIB.SALARY, that you want to create. The VLIB libref must be associated with a SAS data library before you can specify it in this statement.

```
s2kpw=mine mode=single;
```
specifies the password, MINE, required to access the data and indicates the database is in the single-user environment.

```
reset all;
```
resets all the items selected for the view descriptor to the default attributes; that is, the SAS variable name is based on the first eight characters of the SYSTEM 2000 item name, while remaining attributes are based on the item's database type and picture specification.

```
unique=yes;
```
specifies unique SAS variable names for items that are selected for the view descriptor. You can only use this statement if you have omitted the ASSIGN statement (or specified a NO value) when creating the access descriptor on which this view is based.

```
select lastname forename c5 c6 c7 c8 c101 c120;
```
selects the items associated with the LASTNAME and FORENAME SAS variable names and with the C-numbers C5, C6, C7, C8, C101, and C120 for inclusion in the view descriptor. Because C-number C120 indicates a record, all the items in that record are selected for the view descriptor. The SELECT statement is required to create the view unless a RENAME, FORMAT, INFORMAT, LENGTH, or BYKEY statement is also specified.

```
subset "departme=corporation
   ob gross pay";
```
specifies you want the view descriptor to include only observations for the CORPORATION department ordered by the amount of gross pay. Using the word WHERE is optional and can be omitted. The WHERE clause is case sensitive and should be enclosed in quotes. Use the SAS/ACCESS interface to SYSTEM 2000 syntax in the SUBSET statement.

```
list view;
```
lists the item identifier numbers, the C-numbers, the SAS variable names, the SAS formats, the SAS informats, and the SAS variable lengths that have been selected for the view descriptor. Any associated BY key information is also listed. Selection criteria specified in the view descriptor are listed. In noninteractive and batch modes, the list is written to the SAS log.

```
run;
```
writes the view descriptor when the RUN statement is processed.

Creating Several View Descriptors

You can create more than one view descriptor in a single PROC ACCESS execution. The following example creates two view descriptors, named

VLIB.DEGREES and VLIB.TRAIN. Each statement is then explained in the order it appears in the example program.

```
proc access dbms=s2k accdesc=mylib.educ;
   create vlib.degrees.view;
      select c2 c3 c141;
      rename c141=title;
      format c8 date9.;
      subset "ob title desc";
      list all;
   create vlib.train.view;
      select c2 c3 c6 c16;
      rename c163=datedone;
      list view;
run;
```

Here is an explanation of the statements in this example:

`proc access dbms=s2k accdesc=mylib.educ;`
> invokes the ACCESS procedure for the SAS/ACCESS interface for SYSTEM 2000 software and specifies that the view descriptors will be created based on the access descriptor MYLIB.EDUC. The MYLIB libref must be associated with a SAS data library before you can specify it in the ACCDESC= option.

`create vlib.degrees.view;`
> identifies the view descriptor, VLIB.DEGREES, that you want to create. The VLIB libref must be associated with a SAS data library before you can specify it in this statement.

`select c2 c3 c141;`
> selects the items associated with C-numbers C2, C3, and C141 for inclusion in the view descriptor.

`rename c141=title;`
> renames the SAS variable associated with C-number C141 to TITLE. Any item that is renamed is automatically included in the view descriptor.

`format c8 date9.`
> assigns the DATE9. format to the item associated with C-number C8. Any item that is reformatted is automatically included in the view descriptor.

`subset "ob title desc";`
> specifies you want the observations for the TITLE variable sorted in descending order. Use the SAS/ACCESS interface to SYSTEM 2000 syntax in the SUBSET statement.

`list all;`
> lists all the available item identifier numbers, C-numbers, SAS variable names, SAS formats, SAS informats, and SAS lengths in the access descriptor on which the view descriptor is based. Any associated BY key information is also listed. Selection criteria specified in the view descriptor are listed. In noninteractive or batch mode, the list is written to the SAS log. Any items that have been dropped from display are not listed.

```
create vlib.train.view;
```
write the previous view descriptor and identifies the next view descriptor, VLIB.TRAIN, that you want to create.

```
select c2 c3 c6 c16;
```
selects the items associated with C-numbers C2, C3, C6, and C16 for inclusion in the view descriptor. Because C-number C16 indicates a record, all the items in that record are selected for the view descriptor.

```
rename c163=datedone;
```
renames the SAS variable associated with C-number C163 to DATEDONE. The item associated with C-number C163 is selected because that item is specified in the RENAME statement.

```
list view;
```
lists the item identifier numbers, C-numbers, SAS variable names, SAS formats, SAS informats, and SAS lengths that have been selected for the view descriptor. Any associated BY key information is also listed. Selection criteria specified in the view descriptor are listed. In noninteractive and batch modes, the list is written to the SAS log.

```
run;
```
writes the last view descriptor when the RUN statement is processed.

Commands

The following section describes the commands that can be issued in the ACCESS window and in the View Descriptor Display window. The commands fall into two types:

□   command-line commands

□   selection-field commands.

There is also a new command, the SELECTALL command, that can be issued in the View Descriptor Display window.

For ease of use, the following command-line and selection-field commands are listed alphabetically.

Command-line Commands for the ACCESS Window

The following commands are valid on the ACCESS window command line:

BACKWARD | UP   scrolls the display backward. UP is the alias for BACKWARD.

BOTTOM   scrolls to the end of the list of SAS files contained in the window.

CANCEL | END   exits the ACCESS procedure. END is the alias for CANCEL.

COPY   copies a member of a SAS data library to another data library. The syntax for this command is

COPY *<source_libref.>member<.type>*
      <destination_libref.>member<.type>

The *libref* argument refers to the SAS data library where the *member* is stored. The *member* argument can be the name of an access descriptor, a catalog, a SAS data set, or a stored program of member *type* ACCESS, CATALOG, DATA, PROGRAM, or VIEW.

A one-level name assumes WORK as the libref and DATA as the member type (unless a default libref or type has been set up with the LIBRARY and MEMTYPE commands, respectively). WORK refers to the SAS System's default temporary data library. A two-level name assumes a type of DATA.

The _ALL_ keyword can be used as the member name or type to copy a group of members. For example, to copy all SAS data sets (of type DATA) from the library MYLIB to the library NEWLIB, you would use:

```
copy mylib._all_.data  newlib
```

If the destination member or library already exists, use the REPLACE command, described later in this section.

You can use the COPY command to copy the data accessed by a SAS data view into a SAS data file (that is, extract the view's data). The following example copies data accessed by a view descriptor into a new SAS data file:

```
copy vlib.usacust.view  mydata.usacust.data
```

If the SAS data view is password-protected, the same password and level of protection apply to the new SAS data file. You do not specify the password when copying the SAS data view, but you may need to supply the password when using the SAS data file, depending on the kind of SAS data view copied and its level of protection. For example, if a READ password is assigned to a view descriptor and you copy its data to a SAS data file, you must supply the password before you are allowed to browse the data in the new data file.

CREATE   creates an access descriptor in display manager mode using windows. The syntax for this command is

CREATE *libref.access-descriptor*.ACCESS

The *libref.access-descriptor*.ACCESS argument it the three-level name that specifies the libref, member name, and member type of ACCESS for the descriptor you want to create. The libref is required in this command. If you want to create a temporary access descriptor, use the

(CREATE continued)

	libref WORK, which refers to the SAS System's default temporary data library.
EXTRACT	extracts data described by a view descriptor, PROC SQL view, or DATA step view and places them in a SAS data file. The syntax for this command is
	EXTRACT *<libref.>view-name* *<libref.>SAS-data-file*
	The *libref.view-name* argument specifies a two-level name (libref and member name) for the view that describes the data you want to extract. The *libref.SAS-data-file* argument specifies a two-level name (libref and member name) for the output SAS data file. If you want to create a temporary data file, use the libref WORK, which refers to the SAS System's default temporary data library.
FORWARD | DOWN	scrolls the display forward. DOWN is the alias for FORWARD.
HELP	obtains help from the SAS System.
LABEL	adds an item to the ACCESS window that displays any SAS data set labels specified using the LABEL= data set option; entering LABEL again removes the labels item from the display.
LIBRARY	limits the display to a particular libref. The syntax for this command is
	LIBRARY *libref* | _ALL_
	ALL displays all librefs; _ALL_ is the window's default display.
LOAD	invokes the DBLOAD procedure in display manager mode and opens the Engine Selection window. This command enables you to use windows to load a SAS data set into a DBMS table. You can specify an optional *DBMS-name* argument to bypass the Engine Selection window and open the DBLOAD Identification window. The syntax for this command is
	LOAD <S2K>
MEMTYPE	limits the display to a member type, for example DATA or CATALOG. The syntax for this command is
	MEMTYPE *type* | _ALL_
	ALL displays all members; _ALL_ is the window's default display.
REPLACE	copies a member of a SAS data library to another data library, overwriting the destination member if it exists. The syntax for this command is

REPLACE <*source_libref.*>*name*<*.type*>
<*destination_libref.*>*name*<*.type*>

The REPLACE command uses the same arguments and defaults as the COPY command; refer to its description earlier in this section for more information.

RESET   redisplays the window. The RESET command resets the library and member types to display all members; it also displays any new members that have been created.

SORT   sorts the display in descending alphabetical order. The syntax for this command is

SORT *argument-1* <*argument-n*>

The values for *argument* can be LIBREF, NAME, and MEMTYPE. The second argument is used when you want to sort within the first argument. Initially, the display is sorted by library and then by member types.

TOP   scrolls to the top of the list of SAS files contained in the window.

Selection-field Commands for the ACCESS Window

The following selection-field commands are available in the ACCESS window. Type a selection-field command in the field in front of the appropriate member and press the ENTER key. All the commands are listed in alphabetic order for ease of use.

Note in the command descriptions that a *SAS data view* can include a view descriptor, PROC SQL view, or DATA step view; references to a *SAS data set* can include a SAS data view and a SAS data file.

B*   (browse data)
can be placed by a SAS data set. It enables you to use the FSBROWSE procedure to browse the data in a SAS data file or the data described by a SAS data view. The B command is equivalent to invoking the FSBROWSE procedure in display manager mode or in interactive line mode with the appropriate DATA= option. With this command you see only one observation of data at a time.

Before you can browse data retrieved through a SAS/ACCESS interface, you must be granted privileges by the DBMS. See your Release 6.06 SAS/ACCESS documentation for more information.

BD   (browse descriptor)
can be placed by either an access descriptor or a view descriptor. It enables you to browse the descriptor's items, SAS names, formats, and so on. For access and view descriptors, items dropped from the display are not listed.

This selection-field command requires SAS/FSP software as well as SAS/ACCESS software.

To browse the view descriptor, you do not need read privileges on the access descriptor that was used to create the view descriptor.

BL* (browse listing)
can be placed by a SAS data set. It enables you to use the FSVIEW procedure to browse the data in a tabular listing similar to that produced by the PRINT procedure. The BL command is equivalent to invoking the FSVIEW procedure in display manager mode or in interactive line mode with the appropriate DATA= option and no MODIFY option specified.

Before you can browse data retrieved through a SAS/ACCESS interface, you must be granted privileges by the DBMS. See your Release 6.06 SAS/ACCESS documentation for more information.

C (contents)
can be placed by a SAS data set. It enables you to browse descriptive information about a SAS data view or browse and edit descriptive information in a SAS data file. This information is similar to what is produced by the CONTENTS procedure.

When you place the C selection-field command next to a SAS data view, the CONTENTS window appears in browse mode. When you place the C command next to a SAS data file, the CONTENTS window appears in edit mode if you have write access to the library. In edit mode, you can type over variable names, formats, informats, and labels to change the current values. To browse or edit additional descriptive information about the SAS data set, move the cursor to the Data Set Attributes field and press ENTER. The Attributes window appears and displays information such as the data set name, engine, date created, date last modified, data set label, and number of observations.

You can issue the following commands in the CONTENTS window:

INDEX CREATE
opens the Index Create window, enabling you to create indexes on variables in the displayed SAS data file. (Refer to Chapter 6 in *SAS Language: Reference, Version 6, First Edition* for more information on SAS indexes.) This command is valid only if the CONTENTS window is opened for editing. You cannot use this command with a SAS data view.

You can issue the following commands in the Index Create window:

END closes the Index Create window.

REVIEW opens the Index Review window to display the SAS indexes already defined for this SAS data file. You can also delete existing indexes in this window.

RUN creates an index on one or more variables after all required information has been specified.

This selection-field command requires SAS/FSP software as well as SAS/ACCESS software.

INDEX REVIEW
:   opens the Index Review window so that you can view the SAS indexes currently defined for the SAS data file. This command is valid only if the CONTENTS window is opened for editing. You can use the D selection-field command in this window to delete any of the listed indexes. You cannot use this command with a SAS data view.

SORT <NAME | ORDER>
:   sorts the variables in the CONTENTS window display; this command affects only the variables' display and not their actual order in a SAS data set. By default, variables are listed in the order they are defined in the SAS data set. Specifying SORT NAME sorts the display by variable names in descending alphabetical order. Specifying SORT ORDER (or SORT alone) restores the original order. This command is valid in the CONTENTS window for any SAS data set.

CV   (create view)
:   can be placed by an access descriptor. It enables you to create a view descriptor based on this access descriptor in display manager mode using windows.

D   (delete member)
:   can be placed by any member in the ACCESS window. It enables you to delete that member. Enter a V and press ENTER at the verification request to complete the deletion. If you do not enter a V, the request to delete is canceled.

    This command deletes the SAS data set or SAS/ACCESS descriptor, not the descriptor's underlying DBMS table or view.

E*   (edit data)
:   can be placed by a view descriptor or SAS data file. It enables you to use the FSEDIT procedure to edit DBMS data (via the view descriptor) or to edit the data in a SAS data file. The E command is equivalent to invoking the FSEDIT procedure in display manager mode or in interactive line mode with the appropriate DATA= option. With this command, you see only one observation of data at a time.

    Before you can update data retrieved through a SAS/ACCESS interface, you must be granted privileges by the DBMS. See your Release 6.06 SAS/ACCESS documentation for more information.

ED   (edit descriptor)
:   can be placed by an access descriptor or view descriptor. It enables you to edit the descriptor's SAS variable names, formats, and so on, to select or drop items, and to change selection criteria. Whether you can change SAS names and formats in the view descriptor depends on the value you gave the ASSIGN statement (in interactive line, noninteractive, or batch mode) or the Assign Names field in the Access Descriptor Identification window (in display manager mode).

EL*   (edit listing)
:   can be placed by a view descriptor or SAS data file. It enables you to

---

This selection-field command requires SAS/FSP software as well as SAS/ACCESS software.

(EL* continued)

use the FSVIEW procedure to edit the data in a tabular listing similar to that produced by the PRINT procedure. When using the EL command next to a view desriptor, you are directly updating DBMS data in a SAS data file. The EL command is equivalent to invoking the FSVIEW procedure in display manager mode or in interactive line mode with the appropriate DATA= option and the MODIFY option specified.

Before you can update data retrieved through a SAS/ACCESS interface, you must be granted privileges by the DBMS. See your Release 6.06 SAS/ACCESS documentation for more information.

PW   (password)
can be placed by an access descriptor, a SAS data set, or a program (member of type PROGRAM) and enables you to assign it an ALTER, READ, or WRITE password.

When you enter the PW command, a window appears prompting you to enter or change a password. New passwords are not displayed as you enter them nor are existing passwords displayed. Issue the END command to save the passwords and return to the ACCESS window.

Note: You must write down or store your passwords elsewhere, because you cannot retrieve them from the SAS System.

When a password-protected SAS data set or stored DATA step program is used in a SAS program, the data set's password may need to be specified by using a SAS data set option, depending on the PW type and the access type, or you will be prompted if you are running the procedure interactively. See "Specifying SAS System Passwords for SAS/ACCESS Descriptors" later in this chapter and SAS Technical Report P-222, *Changes and Enhancements to Base SAS Software, Release 6.07* for more information on and examples of using passwords.

R   (rename member)
can be placed by any member and enables you to rename that member. Press ENTER, type the new name over the existing member name, and press ENTER again. This command renames the data set or descriptor, not the descriptor's underlying table or view.

▶ *Caution* . . . . *Be careful when you rename an access descriptor, because the view descriptors associated with it are no longer linked to it.* ▲

?   can be placed by any member. It displays a window that describes all the selection-field commands and enables you to select any of the selection-field commands.

Command-line Command for the View Descriptor Display Window

A new command, the SELECTALL command, can now be issued from the View Descriptor Display window. The SELECTALL command enables you to select all database columns for your view descriptor.

Use of the SELECTALL command may select fields in more than one path. Attempting to create a view with more than one path will fail with an error message.

Understanding the Flattened File Concept

When the SYSTEM 2000 engine creates SAS observations from a hierarchical database, it may flatten out the data across record levels. That is, if any parent record in the view has children in the view, data in the parent record are repeated in the observation for each child record's data. This is called the *flattened file concept* because the SAS System flattens the hierarchical levels, treating as one SAS observation data from the child record and any participating parent records. This means that each observation will contain data from the parent records above the child record. Figure 2.1 illustrates this concept.

Note: Figure 2.1 uses SAS names in the form SNC*nnn*, where SN stands for the SAS name and C*nnn* stands for a specific C-number.

Figure 2.1   *Flattened File Concept*

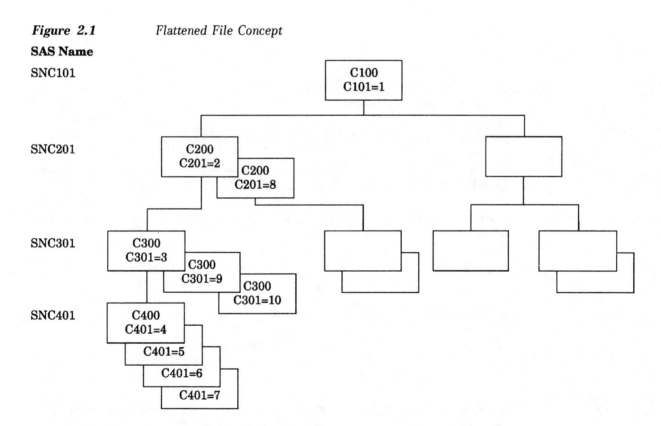

Figure 2.1 shows actual data values; that is, the value of the first occurrence of C-number 201 (C201) is 2 and the second occurrence is 8.

If you access the data in the database shown in Figure 2.1, the SYSTEM 2000 engine returns the following data values as SAS observations:

```
Observation          Data Returned


              SNC101   SNC201   SNC301   SNC401

    1            1        2        3        4
    2            1        2        3        5
    3            1        2        3        6
    4            1        2        3        7
    5            1        8        9        .
    6            1        8       10        .
```

Retrieving Data from Flattened Files

The following section describes how to retrieve data from flattened files correctly, so that you do not receive misleading statistics.

If you use the data from these observations in a SAS procedure, it appears that the data in the level-zero record occur four times, rather than only once as they really do. This can result in misleading statistics when you use such procedures as the MEANS procedure involving data from any record except the child record in a database with more than one hierarchical level. To avoid misleading statistics resulting from flattened files, create view descriptors that describe data in one hierarchical level only or perform statistical operations using only data from the lowest level in the view descriptor.

Updating Data in Flattened Files

The following section describes information you need to understand to update data in flattened files correctly.

Assume you are positioned on observation 1 in FSEDIT, and change the data value of SNC101 from 1 to 11. If you now move to observation 2, the data values have become the following:

```
Observation          Data Returned


              SNC101   SNC201   SNC301   SNC401

    2           11        2        3        5
```

Assume you have the original six observations, and the SAS names shown previously. Submitting the following DATA step should change the values of SNC101 to 11 and the values of SNC401 to 99:

```
data work.mydata;
   modify work.mydata;
   if snc101=1 then
      do;
         snc101=11;
```

```
        snc401=99;
    end;
```

If WORK.MYDATA refers to a SAS data set, then the following data values are returned:

```
Observation         Data Returned

                 SNC101  SNC201  SNC301  SNC401

     1             11       2       3      99
     2             11       2       3      99
     3             11       2       3      99
     4             11       2       3      99
     5             11       8       9      99
     6             11       8      10      99
```

If WORK.MYDATA refers to a view descriptor for a SYSTEM 2000 database, the SYSTEM 2000 engine returns the following data values:

```
Observation         Data Returned

                 SNC101  SNC201  SNC301  SNC401

     1             11       2       3      99
     2             11       2       3       5
     3             11       2       3       6
     4             11       2       3       7
     5             11       8       9       .
     6             11       8      10       .
```

After the value of SNC101 in observation 1 has been changed to 11, the remaining observations have SNC101 values of 11 (not 1). Thus, the following condition fails:

```
if SNC101=1
```

The SNC401 values in these observations are not updated.

Specifying SAS System Passwords for SAS/ACCESS Descriptors

Release 6.07 of the SAS System enables you to control access to SAS data sets and access descriptors by associating one or more SAS System passwords with them. You can assign a password to a descriptor by using the ACCESS window in display manager mode or by using the DATASETS procedure. For either method, you must first create the descriptor.

Note: In the ACCESS procedure, you cannot add a password data set option to the CREATE statement to assign a password while a descriptor is being created. SAS data set options are used with access and view descriptors to specify an existing password.

Table 2.1 summarizes the levels of protection that SAS System passwords have and their effects on access descriptors and view descriptors.

Table 2.1
Password and
Descriptor
Interaction

Descriptor	READ=	WRITE=	ALTER=
access descriptor	no effect on descriptor	no effect on descriptor	protects descriptor from being read or edited
view descriptor	no effect on descriptor	no effect on descriptor	protects descriptor from being read or edited

For detailed information on the levels of protection and the types of passwords you can use, refer to SAS Technical Report P-222. The following section describes how you assign SAS System passwords to descriptors in the four processing modes.

Assigning Passwords

To assign a password to an access descriptor, view descriptor, or other SAS file in display manager mode, you can use the PW command in the ACCESS window. You can also use this command to change passwords. The PW selection-field command is described earlier in this chapter in "Selection-field Commands for the ACCESS Window."

To assign or change a password in interactive line, noninteractive, or batch mode, you use the DATASETS procedure's MODIFY statement. Here is the basic syntax for assigning a password to an access descriptor or a view descriptor:

PROC DATASETS LIBRARY=*libref* MEMTYPE=*member-type*;
    MODIFY *descriptor-name* (*password-level*=*password-modification*);
RUN;

In this syntax statement, the *password-level* argument can have one of the following values: ALTER=, PW=, READ=, or WRITE=. The *password-modification* argument enables you to assign a new password, delete a password, or change passwords. See SAS Technical Report P-222 for all the possible combinations in this argument and for other details.

The following example assigns a password to the MYLIB.ORDERS access descriptor:

```
proc datasets library=mylib memtype=access;
    modify invoice(alter=gelb);
run;
```

▶ *Caution* . . . . *Be careful when using hierarchical databases.*

If your view descriptor contains several record types or levels, then an update to root information in an observation can change data in related observations. If you are using the MODIFY statement within a loop in a DATA step, this can have unforeseen consequences. ▲

Refer to SAS Technical Report P-222 for more examples of assigning, deleting, and using SAS System passwords.

Chapter 3 SAS/ACCESS® Interface to ADABAS Data Management Software

Introduction

This chapter describes the Release 6.07 changes and enhancements for the SAS/ACCESS interface to ADABAS data management software.

Few changes have been made since the publication of *SAS/ACCESS Interface to ADABAS: Usage and Reference, Version 6, First Edition.* The changes fall into three categories:

□ changes to SAS system options

□ changes to the ACCESS procedure

□ changes to the WHERE clause.

The interactive line, noninteractive, and batch mode syntax described in earlier chapters does not apply to the SAS/ACCESS interface to ADABAS.

Also, Release 6.07 provides a SAS System password capability. You can assign passwords to access descriptors and to any kind of SAS data set. This chapter briefly describes how to assign passwords to access and view descriptors.

SAS System Options

SAS system options are described in Appendix 1, "Information for the Database Administrator," of *SAS/ACCESS Interface to ADABAS*. In Release 6.07 of the interface, the following changes apply:

□ the way in which options are specified has changed

□ the ADBENGMD option has been renamed to ADBUPD

□ the ADBTASK option has been added.

These changes are described in the following sections.

System Option Changes

SAS system options for the ADABAS interface are now specified the same way as other SAS system options. The ADABAS options are invocation options. Thus, you can specify the options in a configuration file or when you invoke the SAS System. (Each SAS system option is followed by an equal sign.) They cannot be changed during the SAS session. See Appendix 1 of *SAS/ACCESS Interface to ADABAS* for more information on SAS system options for ADABAS. The ADBAUSE and ADBEUSE CSECTS (assembler language constant sections) described in Appendix 1 are now obsolete.

Several system options can also be specified as data set options. In this case, a data set option value can override a system option for the duration of a single procedure or DATA step. See Appendix 2, "Advanced User Topics," in *SAS/ACCESS Interface to ADABAS* for more information on SAS data set options.

Several system options control the default values used when creating a new access descriptor. You can override the default values by specifying different values in the ACCESS procedure windows or by setting appropriate values to options.

Here are some examples of setting system options for the interface:

```
ADBDBID=2
ADBSYSFL=8
ADBNATAP=DEMO
ADBSYSCC=13579
```

In these examples, ADBDBID=2 specifies the value 2 for the database number containing ADABAS files, ADBSYSFL=8 specifies the file number 8 for the system file, ADBNATAP=DEMO specifies the NATURAL SECURITY system application identifier, and ADBSYSCC=13579 specifies the 13579 cipher code for the system file.

Once your SAS session is executing, you can display the values of system options by entering the following SAS statements:

```
proc options adb;
run;
```

The system options for the SAS/ACCESS interface to ADABAS are written to the SAS log. Note that you cannot see the options for any passwords or cipher codes, as these are hidden from view.

For convenience, you may want to set certain options during installation rather than with each SAS invocation. In addition, you may want to restrict certain options so they cannot be changed for a SAS session. You do this by specifying their values in the Restricted Options Table during installation. Refer to the installation instructions for details.

To access online information describing each option, you can enter the following command from the command line during a SAS session:

```
help options
```

The SAS SYSTEM HELP: OPTIONS Selection window displays. In this window, move the cursor to **Host Options** and press the ENTER key. The MVS HELP window appears. In the MVS HELP window, move the cursor to **Configuration** under `System Options`, and press ENTER. The MVS HELP: System Configuration Options window appears. In this window, select **ADB*** (where the asterisk indicates any option name beginning with ADB), and the MVS HELP: The ADB* System Options window appears. This window provides a separate display for each ADABAS system option, its syntax, and possible values.

ADBENGMD Option Renamed

The ADBENGMD option has been renamed the ADBUPD option. This option determines whether the interface view engine is allowed to perform updates against ADABAS tables. The value **Y** allows update; the value **N** allows read-only access. When the value is **N**, any attempt to update an ADABAS database is rejected and an error message is written to the SAS log.

The default value is Y.

New ADBTASK Option

The new ADBTASK option determines whether the SAS/ACCESS engine for ADABAS operates in a single-task or multiple-task mode. In single-task mode, the ADABAS engine represents itself as one task to the ADABAS multi-user address space.

In multiple-task mode, the ADABAS engine initiates an ADABAS multi-user task for each active window or open file. You should use multiple-task mode in the following cases:

□ when the ADABAS engine resides in the SAS/SHARE address space

□ when SAS/ASSIST software is used, especially for graphics

□ when you activate multiple editing windows in one session

□ when you define PROC SQL views that join multiple files.

The values for the ADBTASK option are S for single and M for multiple. The default is S. To change the option to M, you must also make some installation changes. The nature of these changes is to modify an assembler program provided by Software AG called UEXITB and to link it with the SAS/ACCESS engine for ADABAS. Contact the SAS Technical Support division for assistance.

Commands

The following section describes the commands that can be issued in the ACCESS window. The commands fall into two categories:

□   command-line commands

□   selection-field commands.

For ease of use, the following command-line and selection-field commands are listed alphabetically.

Command-line Commands for the ACCESS Window

The following commands are valid on the ACCESS window command line:

BACKWARD | UP   scrolls the display backward. UP is the alias for BACKWARD.

BOTTOM   scrolls to the end of the list of SAS files contained in the window.

CANCEL | END   exits the ACCESS procedure. END is the alias for CANCEL.

COPY   copies a member of a SAS data library to another data library. The syntax for this command is

COPY <*source_libref.*>*member*<.*type*>
    <*destination_libref.*>*member*<.*type*>

The *libref* argument refers to the SAS data library where the *member* is stored. The *member* argument can be the name of an access descriptor, a catalog, a SAS data set, or a stored program of member *type* ACCESS, CATALOG, DATA, PROGRAM, or VIEW.

A one-level name assumes WORK as the libref and DATA as the member type (unless a default libref or type has been set up with the LIBRARY and MEMTYPE commands, respectively). WORK refers to the SAS System's default temporary data library. A two-level name assumes a type of DATA.

The _ALL_ keyword can be used as the member name or type to copy a group of members. For example, to copy all SAS data sets (of type DATA) from the library MYLIB to the library NEWLIB, you would use:

```
copy mylib._all_.data  newlib
```

If the destination member or library already exists, use the REPLACE command, described later in this section.

You can use the COPY command to copy the data accessed by a SAS data view into a SAS data file (that is, extract the view's data). The following example copies data accessed by a view descriptor into a new SAS data file:

```
copy vlib.usacust.view  mydata.usacust.data
```

If the SAS data view is password-protected, the same password and level of protection apply to the new SAS data file. You do not specify the password when copying the SAS data view, but you may need to supply the password when using the SAS data file, depending on the kind of SAS data view copied and its level of protection. For example, if a read password is assigned to a view descriptor and you copy its data to a SAS data file, you must supply the password before you are allowed to browse the data in the new data file.

CREATE

creates an access descriptor in display manager mode using windows. The syntax for this command is

CREATE *libref.access-descriptor*.ACCESS

The *libref.access-descriptor*.ACCESS argument is the three-level name that specifies the libref, member name, and member type of ACCESS for the descriptor you want to create. The libref is required in this command. If you want to create a temporary access descriptor, use the libref WORK, which refers to the SAS System's default temporary data library.

EXTRACT

extracts data described by a view descriptor, PROC SQL view, or DATA step view and places them in a SAS data file. The syntax for this command is

EXTRACT <*libref.*>*view-name* <*libref.*>*SAS-data-file*

The *libref.view-name* argument specifies a two-level name (libref and member name) for the view that describes the data you want to extract. The *libref.SAS-data-file* argument specifies a two-level name (libref and member name) for the output SAS data file. If you want to create a temporary data file, use the libref WORK, which refers to the SAS System's default temporary data library.

FORWARD | DOWN

scrolls the display forward. DOWN is the alias for FORWARD.

HELP

obtains help from the SAS System.

LABEL

adds a data field to the ACCESS window that displays any SAS data set labels specified using the LABEL= data set option; entering LABEL again removes the labels data field from the display.

LIBRARY

limits the display to a particular libref. The syntax for this command is

LIBRARY *libref* | _ALL_

ALL displays all librefs; _ALL_ is the window's default display.

MEMTYPE

limits the display to a member type, for example, DATA or CATALOG. The syntax for this command is

MEMTYPE *type* | _ALL_

ALL displays all members; _ALL_ is the window's default display.

REPLACE

copies a member of a SAS data library to another data library, overwriting the destination member if it exists. The syntax for this command is

REPLACE <*source_libref.*>*name*<*.type*>
        <*destination_libref.*>*name*<*.type*>

The REPLACE command uses the same arguments and defaults as the COPY command; refer to its description earlier in this section for more information.

RESET

redisplays the window. The RESET command resets the library and member types to display all members; it also displays any new members that have been created.

SORT

sorts the display in descending alphabetical order. The syntax for this command is

SORT *argument-1* <*argument-n*>

The values for *argument* can be LIBREF, NAME, and MEMTYPE. The second argument is used when you want to sort within the first argument. Initially, the display is sorted by library and then by member types.

TOP

scrolls to the top of the list of SAS files contained in the window.

Selection-field Commands for the ACCESS Window

The following selection-field commands are available in the ACCESS window. Type a selection-field command in the field in front of the appropriate member and press the ENTER key. All the commands are listed in alphabetic order for ease of use.

Note in the command descriptions that a *SAS data view* can include a view descriptor, PROC SQL view, or DATA step view; references to a *SAS data set* can include a SAS data view and a SAS data file.

B*   (browse data)

can be placed by a SAS data set. It enables you to use the FSBROWSE procedure to browse the data in a SAS data file or the data described by a SAS data view. The B command is equivalent to invoking the FSBROWSE procedure in display manager mode or in interactive line mode with the appropriate DATA= option. With this command you see only one observation of data at a time.

Before you can browse data retrieved through a SAS/ACCESS interface, you must be granted privileges by the DBMS. See your Release 6.06 SAS/ACCESS documentation for more information.

BD   (browse descriptor)

can be placed by either an access descriptor or a view descriptor. It enables you to browse the descriptor's data fields, SAS names, formats, and so on. For access and view descriptors, data fields dropped from the display are not listed.

To browse the view descriptor, you do not need read privileges on the access descriptor that was used to create the view descriptor.

BL*   (browse listing)

can be placed by a SAS data set. It enables you to use the FSVIEW procedure to browse the data in a tabular listing similar to that produced by the PRINT procedure. The BL command is equivalent to invoking the FSVIEW procedure in display manager mode or in interactive line mode with the appropriate DATA= option and no MODIFY option specified.

Before you can browse data retrieved through a SAS/ACCESS interface, you must be granted privileges by the DBMS. See your Release 6.06 SAS/ACCESS documentation for more information.

C   (contents)

can be placed by a SAS data set. It enables you to browse descriptive information about a SAS data view or browse and edit descriptive information in a SAS data file. This information is similar to what is produced by the CONTENTS procedure.

When you place the C selection-field command next to a SAS data view, the CONTENTS window appears in browse mode. When you place the C command next to a SAS data file, the CONTENTS window appears in edit mode if you have write access to the library. In edit mode, you can type over variable names, formats, informats, and labels to change the current values. To browse or edit additional descriptive information about the SAS data set, move the cursor to the Data Set Attributes field and press ENTER. The Attributes window appears and displays information such as the data set name, engine, date created, date last modified, data set label, and number of observations.

You can issue the following commands in the CONTENTS window:

This selection-field command requires SAS/FSP software as well as SAS/ACCESS software.

INDEX CREATE
: opens the Index Create window, enabling you to create indexes on variables in the displayed SAS data file. (Refer to Chapter 6 in *SAS Language: Reference, Version 6, First Edition* for more information on SAS indexes.) This command is valid only if the CONTENTS window is opened for editing. You cannot use this command with a SAS data view.

  You can issue the following commands in the Index Create window:

END
: closes the Index Create window.

REVIEW
: opens the Index Review window to display the SAS indexes already defined for this SAS data file. You can also delete existing indexes in this window.

RUN
: creates an index on one or more variables after all required information has been specified.

INDEX REVIEW
: opens the Index Review window so that you can view the SAS indexes currently defined for the SAS data file. This command is valid only if the CONTENTS window is opened for editing. You can use the D selection-field command in this window to delete any of the listed indexes. You cannot use this command with a SAS data view.

SORT <NAME | ORDER>
: sorts the variables in the CONTENTS window display; this command affects only the variables' display and not their actual order in a SAS data set. By default, variables are listed in the order they are defined in the SAS data set. Specifying SORT NAME sorts the display by variable names in descending alphabetical order. Specifying SORT ORDER (or SORT alone) restores the original order. This command is valid in the CONTENTS window for any SAS data set.

CV
: (create view)
  can be placed by an access descriptor. It enables you to create a view descriptor based on this access descriptor in display manager mode using windows.

D
: (delete member)
  can be placed by any member in the ACCESS window. It enables you to delete that member. Enter a V and press ENTER at the verification request to complete the deletion. If you do not enter a V, the request to delete is canceled.

  This command deletes the SAS data set or SAS/ACCESS descriptor, not the descriptor's underlying DBMS table or view.

E*   (edit data)
      can be placed by a view descriptor or a SAS data file. It enables you to
      use the FSEDIT procedure to edit DBMS data (via the view descriptor)
      or to edit the data in a SAS data file. The E command is equivalent to
      invoking the FSEDIT procedure in display manager mode or in
      interactive line mode with the appropriate DATA= option. With this
      command, you see only one observation of data at a time.
           Before you can update data retrieved through a SAS/ACCESS
      interface, you must be granted privileges by the DBMS. See your Release
      6.06 SAS/ACCESS documentation for more information.

ED   (edit descriptor)
      can be placed by an access descriptor or view descriptor. It enables you
      to edit the descriptor's SAS variable names, formats, and so on, to select
      or drop data fields, and to change selection criteria. Whether you can
      change SAS names and formats in the view descriptor depends on the
      value you gave the ASSIGN statement (in interactive line, noninteractive,
      or batch mode) or the Assign Names field in the Access Descriptor
      Identification window (in display manager mode).

EL*   (edit listing)
      can be placed by a view descriptor or a SAS data file. file. It enables you
      to use the FSVIEW procedure to edit the data in a tabular listing similar
      to that produced by the PRINT procedure. When using the EL command
      next to a view descriptor, you are directly updating DBMS data in a SAS
      data file. The EL command is equivalent to invoking the FSVIEW
      procedure in display manager mode or in interactive line mode with the
      appropriate DATA= option and the MODIFY option specified.
           Before you can update data retrieved through a SAS/ACCESS
      interface, you must be granted privileges by the DBMS. See your Release
      6.06 SAS/ACCESS documentation for more information.

PW   (password)
      can be placed by an access descriptor, a SAS data set, or a program
      (member of type PROGRAM) and enables you to assign it an ALTER,
      READ, or WRITE password.
           When you enter the PW command, a window appears prompting
      you to enter or change a password. New passwords are not displayed as
      you enter them nor are existing passwords displayed. Issue the END
      command to save the passwords and return to the ACCESS window.
           Note: You must write down or store your passwords elsewhere,
      because you cannot retrieve them from the SAS System.
           When a password-protected SAS data set or stored DATA step
      program is used in a SAS program, the data set's password may need to
      be specified by using a SAS data set option, depending on the PW type
      and the access type, or you will be prompted if you are running the
      procedure interactively. See "Specifying SAS System Passwords for
      SAS/ACCESS Descriptors" later in this chapter and SAS Technical
      Report P-222, *Changes and Enhancements to Base SAS Software, Release
      6.07* for more information on and examples of using passwords.

This selection-field command requires SAS/FSP software as well as SAS/ACCESS software.

R   (rename member)
can be placed by any member and enables you to rename that member. Press ENTER, type the new name over the existing member name, and press ENTER again. This command renames the data set or descriptor, not the descriptor's underlying table or view.

▶ *Caution* . . . . *Be careful when you rename an access descriptor, because the view descriptors associated with it are no longer linked to it.* ▲

?   can be placed by any member. It displays a window that describes all the selection-field commands and enables you to select any of the selection-field commands.

ACCESS Procedure Changes

The following changes have been made to the ACCESS procedure:

□ creating a temporary access descriptor in the ACCESS Descriptor Identification window has changed

□ the View Descriptor Display window has been changed and the SELECTALL command has been added to this window

□ WHERE clause rules for subdescriptors have changed.

Access Descriptor Identification Changes

The way to create a temporary access descriptor in the Access Descriptor Identification window has changed. To create a temporary access descriptor, specify the libref WORK in the CREATE command that you enter from the ACCESS window. WORK refers to the SAS System's default temporary data library and is displayed in the Library field of the Access Descriptor Identification window.

View Descriptor Display Window Changes

If a user is looking at the View Descriptor Display window and a duplicate SAS name is found in the expansion of a multiple valued field, the name field of the multiple valued field is highlighted. The user can then enter the 'o' function code to invoke the Occurs window and then change the duplicate SAS name.

SELECTALL Command Added

The SELECTALL command has been added to the View Descriptor Display and Occurs windows. The SELECTALL command enables you to select all ADABAS data fields for your view descriptor from the View Descriptor Display window. The SELECTALL command also applies to the Occurs window.

WHERE Clause Changes

Values for numeric ADABAS subdescriptors in view descriptor WHERE clauses must be specified in character hexadecimal. For example, if ZIPLAST2 is a numeric subdescriptor referring to the last two digits of an unpacked ADABAS field, then the following WHERE clause in a view descriptor specifies the value 01:

```
where ziplast2=F0F1
```

For a SAS WHERE clause, specify the following:

```
where ziplast2=01
```

Specifying SAS System Passwords for SAS/ACCESS Descriptors

You can assign SAS System passwords to a view descriptor, access descriptor, PROC SQL view, DATA step view, or data file. In the current release of the SAS System, you can assign

□ the READ, WRITE, and ALTER passwords to a view descriptor, access descriptor, PROC SQL view, DATA step view, or data file using the PW selection-field command in the ACCESS window

□ the READ, WRITE, ALTER, and PW passwords to an existing access or view descriptor, PROC SQL view, DATA step view, or data file using the MODIFY statement of the DATASETS procedure.

Refer to "Selection-field Commands for the ACCESS Window" earlier in this chapter for more information on the PW selection-field command.

Using passwords adds an extra measure of security if you are using view descriptors that include sensitive or confidential data in a shared environment (that is, where SAS/SHARE software is in use). For more information on assigning passwords to a view descriptor, refer to SAS Technical Report P-222, *Changes and Enhancements to Base SAS Software, Release 6.07.*

Release 6.07 of the SAS System enables you to control access to SAS data sets and access descriptors by associating one or more SAS System passwords with them. You can assign a password to a descriptor by using the ACCESS window in display manager mode or by using the DATASETS procedure. For either method, you must first create the descriptor.

Note: In the ACCESS procedure, you cannot add a password data set option to the CREATE statement to assign a password while a descriptor is being created. SAS data set options are used with access and view descriptors to specify an existing password.

Table 3.1 summarizes the levels of protection that SAS System passwords have and their effects on access descriptors and view descriptors.

Table 3.1
Password and
Descriptor
Interaction

Descriptor	READ=	WRITE=	ALTER=
access descriptor	no effect on descriptor	no effect on descriptor	protects descriptor from being read or edited
view descriptor	no effect on descriptor	no effect on descriptor	protects descriptor from being read or edited

For detailed information on the levels of protection and the types of passwords you can use, refer to SAS Technical Report P-222. The following section describes how you assign SAS System passwords to descriptors in the four processing modes.

Assigning Passwords

To assign a password to an access descriptor, view descriptor, or other SAS file in display manager mode, you can use the PW command in the ACCESS window. You can also use this command to change passwords. The PW selection-field command is described earlier in this chapter in "Selection-field Commands for the ACCESS Window."

To assign or change a password in interactive line, noninteractive, or batch mode, you use the DATASETS procedure's MODIFY statement. Here is the basic syntax for assigning a password to an access descriptor or a view descriptor:

PROC DATASETS LIBRARY=*libref* MEMTYPE=*member-type*;
   MODIFY *descriptor-name* (*password-level*=*password-modification*);
RUN;

In this syntax statement, the *password-level* argument can have one of the following values: ALTER=, PW=, READ=, or WRITE=. The *password-modification* argument enables you to assign a new password, delete a password, or change passwords. See SAS Technical Report P-222 for all the possible combinations in this argument and for other details.

The following example assigns a password to the MYLIB.ORDERS access descriptor:

```
proc datasets library=mylib memtype=access;
   modify invoice(alter=gelb);
run;
```

Refer to SAS Technical Report P-222 for more examples of assigning, deleting, and using SAS System passwords.

Chapter 4 SAS/ACCESS® Interface to CA-DATACOM/DB Data Management Software

Introduction

This chapter describes the Release 6.07 changes and enhancements for the SAS/ACCESS interface to CA-DATACOM/DB data management software.

Few changes have been made since the publication of *SAS/ACCESS Interface to CA-DATACOM/DB: Usage and Reference, Version 6, First Edition*. The changes fall into three categories:

☐ changes to SAS system options

☐ changes to the ACCESS procedure

☐ changes to the SQL procedure.

The interactive line, noninteractive, and batch mode syntax described in earlier chapters does not apply to the SAS/ACCESS interface to CA-DATACOM/DB.

Also, Release 6.07 provides a SAS System password capability. You can assign passwords to access descriptors and to any kind of SAS data set. This chapter briefly describes how to assign passwords to access and view descriptors.

SAS System Options

SAS system options are described in Appendix 1, "Information for the Database Administrator," of *SAS/ACCESS Interface to CA-DATACOM/DB*. In Release 6.07 of the interface, the following changes apply:

□ the way in which options are specified has changed

□ the DDBENGMD option has been renamed to DDBUPD.

These changes are described in the following sections.

System Option Changes

SAS system options for the CA-DATACOM/DB interface are now specified the same way as other SAS system options. The CA-DATACOM/DB options are invocation options. Thus, you can specify the options in a configuration file, in the DFLTOPTS table, or when you invoke the SAS System. (Each SAS system option is followed by an equal sign.) They cannot be changed during the SAS session. See Appendix 1 of *SAS/ACCESS Interface to CA-DATACOM/DB* for more information on SAS system options for CA-DATACOM/DB. The DDBAUSE and DDBEUSE CSECTS (assembler language constant sections) described in Appendix 1 are now obsolete.

Several system options (for example, DDBDBN=, DDBPW=, DDBUSER=, and DDBSV=) can also be specified as data set options. In this case, a data set option value can override a system option for the duration of a single procedure or DATA step. See Appendix 2, "Advanced User Topics," in *SAS/ACCESS Interface to CA-DATACOM/DB* for information on SAS data set options.

Several system options control the default values used when creating a new access descriptor. You can override the default values by specifying different values in the ACCESS procedure windows or by setting the appropriate values to the options.

Here are some examples of setting system options for the interface:

```
DDBDBN=INVENTORY
DDBLOAD=1
```

The first system option sets INVENTORY to be the CA-DATACOM/DB name shown in the ACCESS procedure. The second system option requests the CA-DATACOM/DB engine to keep track of the number of inserts to the database.

Once your SAS session is executing, you can display the values of system options by entering the following SAS statements:

```
proc options ddb;
run;
```

The system options for the SAS/ACCESS interface to CA-DATACOM/DB are written to the SAS log. Note that you cannot see the options for any passwords.

For convenience, you may want to set certain options during installation rather than with each SAS invocation. In addition, you may want to restrict certain options so they cannot be changed for a SAS session. You do this by specifying their values in the Restricted Options Table during installation. Refer to the installation instructions for details.

To access online information describing each option, you can enter the following command from the command line during a SAS session:

```
help options
```

The SAS SYSTEM HELP: OPTIONS Selection window displays. In this window, move the cursor to **Host Options** and press the ENTER key. The MVS HELP window appears. In the MVS HELP window, move the cursor to **Configuration** under `System Options`, and press ENTER. The MVS HELP: System Configuration Options window appears. In this window, select **DDB*** (where the asterisk indicates any option name beginning with DDB), and the MVS HELP: The DDB* System Options window appears. This window provides a separate display for each CA-DATACOM/DB system option, its syntax, and possible values.

DDBENGMD Option Renamed

The DDBENGMD option has been renamed the DDBUPD option. This option determines whether the interface view engine is allowed to perform updates against the CA-DATACOM/DB tables. The value **Y** allows updates; the value **N** allows read-only access. When the value is **N**, any attempt to update a CA-DATACOM/DB table is rejected and an error message is written to the SAS log.

The default value is Y.

Commands

The following section describes the commands that can be issued in the ACCESS window. The commands fall into two categories:

❑ command-line commands

❑ selection-field commands.

For ease of use, the following command-line and selection-field commands are listed alphabetically.

Command-line Commands for the ACCESS Window

The following commands are valid on the ACCESS window command line:

BACKWARD | UP   scrolls the display backward. UP is the alias for BACKWARD.

BOTTOM   scrolls to the end of the list of SAS files contained in the window.

CANCEL | END

exits the ACCESS procedure. END is the alias for CANCEL.

COPY

copies a member of a SAS data library to another data library. The syntax for this command is

COPY <*source_libref.*>*member*<*.type*>
      <*destination_libref.*>*member*<*.type*>

The *libref* argument refers to the SAS data library where the *member* is stored. The *member* argument can be the name of an access descriptor, a catalog, a SAS data set, or a stored program of member *type* ACCESS, CATALOG, DATA, VIEW, or PROGRAM.

A one-level name assumes WORK as the libref and DATA as the member type (unless a default libref or type has been set up with the LIBRARY and MEMTYPE commands, respectively). WORK refers to the SAS System's default temporary data library. A two-level name assumes a type of DATA.

The _ALL_ keyword can be used as the member name or type to copy a group of members. For example, to copy all SAS data sets (of type DATA) from the library MYLIB to the library NEWLIB, you would use:

```
copy mylib._all_.data  newlib
```

If the destination member or library already exists, use the REPLACE command, described later in this section.

You can use the COPY command to copy the data accessed by a SAS data view into a SAS data file (that is, extract the view's data). The following example copies data accessed by a view descriptor into a new SAS data file:

```
copy vlib.usacust.view mydata.usacust.data
```

If the SAS data view is password-protected, the same password and level of protection apply to the new SAS data file. You do not specify the password when copying the SAS data view, but you may need to supply the password when using the SAS data file, depending on the kind of SAS data view copied and its level of protection. For example, if a read password is assigned to a view descriptor and you copy its data to a SAS data file, you must supply the password before you are allowed to browse the data in the new data file.

CREATE

creates an access descriptor in display manager mode using windows. The syntax for this command is

CREATE *libref.access-descriptor*.ACCESS

The *libref.access-descriptor* .ACCESS argument is the three-level name that specifies the libref, member name, and member type of ACCESS for the descriptor you want to create. The libref is required in this command. If you want to create a temporary access descriptor, use the libref WORK, which refers to the SAS System's default temporary data library.

EXTRACT

extracts data described by a view descriptor, PROC SQL view, or DATA step view and places them in a SAS data file. The syntax for this command is

EXTRACT *<libref.>view-name   <libref.>SAS-data-file*

The *libref.view-name* argument specifies a two-level name (libref and member name) for the view that describes the data you want to extract. The *libref.SAS-data-file* argument specifies a two-level name (libref and member name) for the output SAS data file. If you want to create a temporary data file, use the libref WORK, which refers to the SAS System's default temporary data library.

FORWARD | DOWN

scrolls the display forward. DOWN is the alias for FORWARD.

HELP

obtains help from the SAS System.

LABEL

adds a field to the ACCESS window that displays any SAS data set labels specified using the LABEL= data set option; entering LABEL again removes the labels field from the display.

LIBRARY

limits the display to a particular libref. The syntax for this command is

LIBRARY *libref* | _ALL_

ALL displays all librefs; _ALL_ is the window's default display.

MEMTYPE

limits the display to a member type, for example, DATA or CATALOG. The syntax for this command is

MEMTYPE *type* | _ALL_

ALL displays all members; _ALL_ is the window's default display.

REPLACE

copies a member of a SAS data library to another data library, overwriting the destination member if it exists. The syntax for this command is

REPLACE *<source_libref.>name<.type>*
       <destination_libref.>name<.type>

The REPLACE command uses the same arguments and defaults as the COPY command; refer to its description earlier in this section for more information.

RESET

redisplays the window. The RESET command resets the library and member types to display all members; it also displays any new members that have been created.

SORT sorts the display in descending alphabetical order. The syntax for this command is

SORT *argument-1* <*argument-n*>

The values for *argument* can be LIBREF, NAME, and MEMTYPE. The second argument is used when you want to sort within the first argument. Initially, the display is sorted by library and then by member types.

TOP scrolls to the top of the list of SAS files contained in the window.

Selection-field Commands for the ACCESS Window

The following selection-field commands are available in the ACCESS window. Type a selection-field command in the field in front of the appropriate member and press the ENTER key. All the commands are listed in alphabetic order for ease of use.

Note in the command descriptions that a *SAS data set* can include a view descriptor, PROC SQL view, or DATA step view; references to a *SAS data set* can include a SAS data view and a SAS data file.

B* (browse data)
can be placed by a SAS data set. It enables you to use the FSBROWSE procedure to browse the data in a SAS data file or the data described by a SAS data view. The B command is equivalent to invoking the FSBROWSE procedure in display manager mode or in interactive line mode with the appropriate DATA= option. With this command you see only one observation of data at a time.

Before you can browse data retrieved through a SAS/ACCESS interface, you must be granted privileges by the DBMS. See your Release 6.06 SAS/ACCESS documentation for more information.

BD (browse descriptor)
can be placed by either an access descriptor or a view descriptor. It enables you to browse the descriptor's fields, SAS names, formats, and so on. For access and view descriptors, fields dropped from the display are not listed.

To browse the view descriptor, you do not need read privileges on the access descriptor that was used to create the view descriptor.

BL* (browse listing)
can be placed by a SAS data set. It enables you to use the FSVIEW procedure to browse the data in a tabular listing similar to that produced by the PRINT procedure. The BL command is equivalent to invoking the FSVIEW procedure in display manager mode or in interactive line mode with the appropriate DATA= option and no MODIFY option specified.

Before you can browse data retrieved through a SAS/ACCESS interface, you must be granted privileges by the DBMS. See your Release 6.06 SAS/ACCESS documentation for more information.

C   (contents)

can be placed by a SAS data set. It enables you to browse descriptive information about a SAS data view or browse and edit descriptive information in a SAS data file. This information is similar to what is produced by the CONTENTS procedure.

When you place the C selection-field command next to a SAS data view, the CONTENTS window appears in browse mode. When you place the C command next to a SAS data file, the CONTENTS window appears in edit mode if you have write access to the library. In edit mode, you can type over variable names, formats, informats, and labels to change the current values. To browse or edit additional descriptive information about the SAS data set, move the cursor to the Data Set Attributes field and press ENTER. The Attributes window appears and displays information such as the data set name, engine, date created, date last modified, data set label, and number of observations.

You can issue the following commands in the CONTENTS window:

INDEX CREATE

opens the Index Create window, enabling you to create indexes on variables in the displayed SAS data file. (Refer to Chapter 6 in *SAS Language: Reference, Version 6, First Edition* for more information on SAS indexes.) This command is valid only if the CONTENTS window is opened for editing. You cannot use this command with a SAS data view.

You can issue the following commands in the Index Create window:

END	closes the Index Create window.
REVIEW	opens the Index Review window to display the SAS indexes already defined for this SAS data file. You can also delete existing indexes in this window.
RUN	creates an index on one or more variables after all required information has been specified.

INDEX REVIEW

opens the Index Review window so that you can view the SAS indexes currently defined for the SAS data file. This command is valid only if the CONTENTS window is opened for editing. You can use the D selection-field command in this window to delete any of the listed indexes. You cannot use this command with a SAS data view.

SORT <NAME | ORDER>

sorts the variables in the CONTENTS window display; this command affects only the variables' display and not their actual order in a SAS data set. By default, variables are listed in the order they are defined in the SAS data set. Specifying SORT NAME sorts the display by variable names in descending alphabetical order. Specifying SORT

(C continued)

ORDER (or SORT alone) restores the original order. This command is valid in the CONTENTS window for any SAS data set.

CV   (create view)
can be placed by an access descriptor. It enables you to create a view descriptor based on this access descriptor in display manager mode using windows.

D   (delete member)
can be placed by any member in the ACCESS window. It enables you to delete that member. Enter a V and press ENTER at the verification request to complete the deletion. If you do not enter a V, the request to delete is canceled.

This command deletes the SAS data set or SAS/ACCESS descriptor, not the descriptor's underlying DBMS table or view.

E*   (edit data)
can be placed by a view descriptor or SAS data file. It enables you to use the FSEDIT procedure to edit DBMS data (via the view descriptor) or to edit the data in a SAS data file. The E command is equivalent to invoking the FSEDIT procedure in display manager mode or in interactive line mode with the appropriate DATA= option. With this command, you see only one observation of data at a time.

Before you can update data retrieved through a SAS/ACCESS interface, you must be granted privileges by the DBMS. See your Release 6.06 SAS/ACCESS documentation for more information.

ED   (edit descriptor)
can be placed by an access descriptor or view descriptor. It enables you to edit the descriptor's SAS variable names, formats, and so on, to select or drop fields, and to change selection criteria. Whether you can change SAS names and formats in the view descriptor depends on the value you gave the ASSIGN statement (in interactive line, noninteractive, or batch mode) or the Assign Names field in the Access Descriptor Identification window (in display manager mode).

EL*   (edit listing)
can be placed by a view descriptor or SAS data file. It enables you to use the FSVIEW procedure to edit the data in a tabular listing similar to that produced by the PRINT procedure. When using the EL command next to a view descriptor, you are directly updating DBMS data in a SAS data file. The EL command is equivalent to invoking the FSVIEW procedure in display manager mode or in interactive line mode with the appropriate DATA= option and the MODIFY option specified.

Before you can update data retrieved through a SAS/ACCESS interface, you must be granted privileges by the DBMS. See your Release 6.06 SAS/ACCESS documentation for more information.

This selection-field command requires SAS/FSP software as well as SAS/ACCESS software.

PW (password)
can be placed by an access descriptor, a SAS data set, or a program (member of type PROGRAM) and enables you to assign it an ALTER, READ, or WRITE password.

When you enter the PW command, a window appears prompting you to enter or change a password. New passwords are not displayed as you enter them nor are existing passwords displayed. Issue the END command to save the passwords and return to the ACCESS window.

Note: You must write down or store your passwords elsewhere, because you cannot retrieve them from the SAS System.

When a password-protected SAS data set or stored DATA step program is used in a SAS program, the data set's password may need to be specified by a SAS data set option, depending on the PW type and access type, or you will be prompted if you are running the procedure interactively. See "Specifying SAS System Passwords for SAS/ACCESS Descriptors" later in this chapter and SAS Technical Report P-222, *Changes and Enhancements to Base SAS Software, Release 6.07* for more information on and examples of using passwords.

R (rename member)
can be placed by any member and enables you to rename that member. Press ENTER, type the new name over the existing member name, and press ENTER again. This command renames the data set or descriptor, not the descriptor's underlying table or view.

▶ *Caution* . . . . *Be careful when you rename an access descriptor, because the view descriptors associated with it are no longer linked to it.* ▲

? can be placed by any member. It displays a window that describes all the selection-field commands and enables you to select any of the selection-field commands.

ACCESS Procedure Changes

The following changes and enhancements have been made to the ACCESS procedure:

☐ creating a temporary access descriptor in the ACCESS Descriptor Identification window has changed

☐ the View Descriptor Display window has been changed and the SELECTALL command has been added to this window.

Access Descriptor Identification Changes

The way to create a temporary access descriptor in the Access Descriptor Identification window has changed. To create a temporary access descriptor, specify the libref WORK in the CREATE command that you enter from the ACCESS window. WORK refer to the SAS System's default temporary data library

and is displayed in the Library field of the Access Descriptor Identification
window.

View Descriptor Display Window Changes

If a user is looking at the View Descriptor Display window and a duplicate SAS
name is found in the expansion of a multiple valued field, the name field of the
multiple valued field is highlighted. The user can then enter the 'o' function and
change the duplicate SAS name.

SELECTALL Command Added

The SELECTALL command has been added to the View Descriptor Display and
Occurs windows. The SELECTALL command enables you to select all
CA-DATACOM/DB data fields for your view descriptor from the View Descriptor
Display window. The SELECTALL command also applies to the Occurs window.

SQL Procedure Changes

The SQL procedure has been modified to support backouts of group updates for
those databases that support member-level locking. CA-DATACOM/DB software
does not support member-level locks. Therefore, if you use the SQL procedure to
update CA-DATACOM/DB records, you must set a new SQL procedure option to
allow it. This option is called UNDO_POLICY. Set the value to NONE for the
CA/DATACOM/DB interface. Here is an example:

```
proc sql undo_policy=none;
update sasuser.usacust
set zipcode=27702
where customer='12345678';
```

If the option is specified, the update is processed. If the update is processed
successfully, it is applied to the database table and a warning message is issued.
The message signifies that if multiple records were updated by the command and a
failure occurred some time after the first record was successfully processed, then
there is no way for PROC SQL to avoid a partial update.

Partial updating means that some records are updated and some are not. It
does not mean that some fields in the same record are updated while other fields
are not.

Specifying SAS System Passwords for SAS/ACCESS Descriptors

You can assign SAS System passwords to a view descriptor, access descriptor,
PROC SQL view, DATA step view, or data file. In Release 6.07 of the SAS
System, you can assign

□ the READ, WRITE, and ALTER passwords to a view descriptor, access
descriptor, PROC SQL view, DATA step view, or data file using the PW
selection-field command in the ACCESS window

□ the READ, WRITE, ALTER, and PW passwords to an existing access or view
descriptor, PROC SQL view, DATA step view, or data file using the MODIFY
statement of the DATASETS procedure.

Refer to "Selection-field Commands for the ACCESS Window" earlier in this
chapter for more information on the PW selection-field command.

Using passwords adds an extra measure of security if you are using view
descriptors that include sensitive or confidential data in a shared environment
(that is, where SAS/SHARE software is in use). For more information on
assigning passwords to a view descriptor, refer to SAS Technical Report P-222,
Changes and Enhancements to Base SAS Software, Release 6.07.

Release 6.07 of the SAS System enables you to control access to SAS data sets
and access descriptors by associating one or more SAS System passwords with
them. You can assign a password to a descriptor by using the ACCESS window in
display manager mode or by using the DATASETS procedure. For either method,
you must first create the descriptor.

Note: In the ACCESS procedure, you cannot add a password data set option
to the CREATE statement to assign a password while a descriptor is being created.
SAS data set options are used with access and view descriptors to specify an
existing password.

Table 4.1 summarizes the levels of protection that SAS System passwords
have and their effects on access descriptors and view descriptors.

Table 4.1
Password and
Descriptor
Interaction

Descriptor	READ=	WRITE=	ALTER=
access descriptor	no effect on descriptor	no effect on descriptor	protects descriptor from being read or edited
view descriptor	no effect on descriptor	no effect on descriptor	protects descriptor from being read or edited

For detailed information on the levels of protection and the types of
passwords you can use, refer to SAS Technical Report P-222. The following
section describes how you assign SAS System passwords to descriptors in the four
processing modes.

Assigning Passwords

To assign a password to an access descriptor, view descriptor, or other SAS file in
display manager mode, you can use the PW command in the ACCESS window.
You can also use this command to change passwords. The PW selection-field
command is described earlier in this chapter in "Selection-field Commands for the
ACCESS Window."

To assign or change a password in interactive line, noninteractive, or batch mode, you use the DATASETS procedure's MODIFY statement. Here is the basic syntax for assigning a password to an access descriptor or a view descriptor:

PROC DATASETS LIBRARY=*libref* MEMTYPE=*member-type*;
  MODIFY *descriptor-name* (*password-level*=*password-modification*);
RUN;

In this syntax statement, the *password-level* argument can have one of the following values: ALTER=, PW=, READ=, or WRITE=. The *password-modification* argument enables you to assign a new password, delete a password, or change passwords. See SAS Technical Report P-222 for all the possible combinations in this argument and for other details.

The following example assigns a password to the MYLIB.ORDERS access descriptor:

```
proc datasets library=mylib memtype=access;
   modify invoice(alter=gelb);
run;
```

Refer to SAS Technical Report P-222 for more examples of assigning, deleting, and using SAS System passwords.

Chapter **5** The SQL Procedure

Introduction

The SQL procedure has been enhanced in Release 6.07 to enable you to establish a connection with a database management system (DBMS) supported by SAS/ACCESS software, send SQL statements to that DBMS, and end the connection. You can then retrieve data from the DBMS using PROC SQL. These are tasks you perform as part of the SQL Pass-Through facility using the CONNECT, EXECUTE, and DISCONNECT statements and the CONNECTION TO component in the FROM clause of a SELECT statement.

See SAS Technical Report P-222, *Changes and Enhancements to Base SAS Software, Release 6.07*, for information on other changes and enhancements to the SQL procedure.

Overview of the SQL Procedure's Pass-Through Facility

The SQL procedure's Pass-Through facility is available with Release 6.07 of the SAS System and enables you to pass DBMS-specific SQL statements directly to a DBMS for processing. The Pass-Through facility uses a SAS/ACCESS interface view engine to connect to the DBMS. Therefore, you must have SAS/ACCESS software for your DBMS to pass SQL statements to it.

Currently, the Pass-Through facility works with the following relational database management systems supported by SAS/ACCESS software:

DB2	Rdb/VMS
ORACLE	SQL/DS

The SQL statements you pass are DBMS-specific. For example, you pass VAX SQL statements to an Rdb/VMS database. The Pass-Through facility's basic syntax is the same for all the DBMSs. Only the statements used to connect to the DBMS and the SQL statements are DBMS-specific.

With the SQL Pass-Through facility, you can perform the following tasks:

❐ establish a connection with the DBMS using a CONNECT statement and terminate the connection with the DISCONNECT statement

❐ retrieve data from the DBMS to be used in a PROC SQL query with the CONNECTION TO component in a SELECT statement's FROM clause

❐ send DBMS-specific SQL statements to the DBMS using the EXECUTE statement.

You can use the Pass-Through facility statements in a PROC SQL query or you can store them in a PROC SQL view. When a query or view is stored, any options specified in the corresponding CONNECT statement are stored too. Thus, when the PROC SQL view is used in a SAS program, the SAS System can establish the appropriate connection to the DBMS.

SQL Pass-Through Facility Statements

The following sections describe the PROC SQL statements and components that comprise the SQL Pass-Through facility. The statements are listed in alphabetic order, followed by the CONNECTION TO component. Examples using these statements and component are shown later in this chapter.

CONNECT Statement

establishes a connection with a DBMS

Syntax

CONNECT TO *dbms-name* <AS *alias*>
         <(*dbms-argument-1=value* . . .<*dbms-argument-n=value*>)>;

Description

The CONNECT statement enables you to establish a connection with a DBMS that is supported by SAS/ACCESS software. You must have SAS/ACCESS software installed on your system to use this PROC SQL statement.

You establish a connection in order to send PROC SQL statements to or retrieve SQL statements from a DBMS. Once you establish a connection, it remains in effect until you issue a DISCONNECT statement or terminate the SQL procedure.

Using the CONNECT statement is optional with some SAS/ACCESS interfaces. If you do not issue a CONNECT statement, an implicit connection is performed when the first EXECUTE statement or CONNECTION TO component is passed to the DBMS. See the following "Database-Definition Arguments" for information on when the CONNECT statement is required.

Arguments

You use the following arguments with the CONNECT statement:

dbms-name

identifies the DBMS that you want to connect to. You can use one of the following values: DB2, ORACLE, RDB, or SQLDS, which refer to the SAS/ACCESS interfaces to DB2, ORACLE, Rdb/VMS, or SQL/DS. You must specify a DBMS name and may specify an optional alias in the CONNECT statement.

alias

specifies an alias that has 1 to 8 characters. The keyword AS must precede the alias. Some DBMSs allow more than one connection. The optional AS clause enables you to name the connections so you can refer to them later.

(dbms-argument-1=value . . .<dbms-argument-n=value>)

specifies DBMS arguments needed for PROC SQL to connect to the DBMS. These arguments are specific to the DBMS and must be enclosed in parentheses. For some databases, these arguments have default values and are therefore optional. The arguments for each database are described in the next section, "Database-Definition Arguments."

Database-Definition Arguments

DBMS-specific information and the definition arguments for each DBMS are described in the following sections.

DB2   Using the CONNECT statement is optional when connecting to DB2. DB2 has one argument you can specify in this statement. It can connect to multiple DB2 systems.

SSID=*subsystem-id*

specifies the DB2 subsystem ID you want to connect to; the ID can be up to four characters long. If you do not specify the SSID= argument, it defaults to the value of the SAS system option DB2SSID=.

ORACLE   Using the CONNECT statement is optional when connecting to ORACLE. ORACLE has four arguments you can specify in this statement. It can connect to multiple databases (both local and remote) and to multiple userids.

BUFFSIZE=*number-of-rows*;

specifies the number of rows to retrieve from an ORACLE table or view with each fetch. Altering the buffer size can enhance performance. Increasing the buffer size requires more memory but reduces the elapsed time and number of I/O operations performed by the SAS System and ORACLE server. The optimal size for BUFFSIZE= depends on the table size and operation to be performed. The default value is 25 rows.

PASSWORD=*ORACLE-password*;

specifies the ORACLE password. If you do not specify an ORACLE password and username, the ORACLE default database logon ID OPS$*sysid* is used. The PASSWORD= argument must be used in conjunction with the USER= argument. PW= and ORAPW= are aliases for the PASSWORD argument.

CONNECT Statement *continued*

PATH ='*ORACLE-path-designation*';
> specifies the ORACLE two-task device driver and driver-specific parameters to use to retrieve data from ORACLE tables or ORACLE views on a local or remote ORACLE system. The PATH= argument is optional; see below for information on its default value.
>
> The format of the *ORACLE-path-designation* argument is as follows:

'@*driver_prefix:driver_and_db_parameters*';

> The *driver_prefix* argument specifies the two-task device driver you want to use. An at sign (@) is required before this argument and a colon (:) after this argument; enclose the entire argument in single quotes. In Release 6.07 of the SAS System running under the VMS operating system, you can use the following values in the *driver_prefix* argument:

2
> specifies the VMS mailbox driver used to access a database on the local system.

D
> specifies the DECnet network services driver to access a local or remote database.

A
> specifies the ORACLE asynchronous driver to access a remote database.

T
> specifies the TCP/IP driver to access a local or remote database.

> The *driver_and_database_parameters* are driver-specific qualifiers. See the ORACLE documentation on each two-task device driver for information on these parameters and qualifiers.
>
> The PATH= argument is optional. If you omit this argument, the following default value is used for the VMS operating system:

```
path='@2:512';
```

This default assumes the VMS mailbox two-task driver has a mailbox size of 512 bytes.

> You can also enter the information provided by the PATH= argument before invoking the SAS System under VMS. You can enter the DCL DEFINE command with the SASORA_PATH logical name from the VMS prompt. The syntax for the SASORA_PATH logical name is similar to that of the PATH= argument:

DEFINE SASORA_PATH '@*driver_prefix:driver_and_db_parameters*'

> The PATH= argument and SASORA_PATH logical name are processed in the following order of precedence:

1. If the PATH= argument is defined, the SAS/ACCESS interface view engine for ORACLE uses the specifications in the PATH= argument even if the SASORA_PATH logical name is defined.

2. If the PATH= argument is not defined, the SAS/ACCESS engine for ORACLE uses specifications in the SASORA_PATH logical name.

3. If neither the PATH= argument nor the SASORA_PATH logical name is defined, the SAS/ACCESS engine for ORACLE defaults to the VMS two-task mailbox driver.

4. If the user specifies the BUFFSIZE= argument, the fetch interval entered by the user is used.

5. If the user omits the BUFFSIZE= argument, the default fetch interval of 25 rows is used.

USER=*ORACLE-user-name*;
    specifies the ORACLE username to use to execute the procedure. If you do not specify an ORACLE username and password, the ORACLE default database logon ID OPS$*sysid* is used. If you specify the USER= argument, you must also specify the PASSWORD= argument.

Rdb/VMS   Using the CONNECT statement is optional when connecting to Rdb/VMS. If you do not issue the CONNECT statement, the Rdb/VMS engine connects to the default database, if you have specified one using the VMS logical name SQL$DATABASE. There can be only one Rdb/VMS connection active at one time; the second CONNECT statement will fail. Rdb/VMS has one argument you can specify in this statement.

DATABASE='*database*';
    indicates the name and physical location of the database that you want to use. This name can be a fully qualified VMS pathname of the database or a VMS logical name that refers to a database. The .RDB file extension in the database name is optional. Include a node name in the database name if you want to retrieve Rdb/VMS data in a remote database. The DATABASE= argument is not required. If it is not specified, the CONNECT statement defaults to connect to the database specified by the logical name SQL$DATABASE, if the logical name has been defined.

SQL/DS   Using the CONNECT statement is optional when connecting to SQL/DS. SQL/DS has two arguments you can specify in this statement.

PASSWORD<=>*SQL/DS-password*
    specifies the SQL/DS password connected to the SQL/DS userid specified in the USER argument. PW and SQLDSPW are aliases for the PASSWORD argument.

USER<=>*SQL/DS-user-name*
    specifies the SQL/DS userid to use to execute the procedure. If you do not issue a USER argument, the userid defaults to your SQL/DS userid. If you specify the USER argument, you must also specify the PASSWORD argument.

Example

The following example connects to the ORACLE database PROD on Rdb/VMS node VAXNOD using ORACLE user Scott and ORACLE password TIGER and assigns an alias to the DBMS name:

```
proc sql;
connect to oracle (user=scott password=tiger
              path='@D:VAXNOD-PROD') as orac1;
```

DISCONNECT Statement

terminates a connection to a DBMS

Syntax

DISCONNECT FROM *dbms-name* | *alias*;

Description

The DISCONNECT statement enables you to end the connection with a DBMS supported by a SAS/ACCESS interface. An implicit COMMIT is performed before the DISCONNECT statement ends the DBMS connection. If a DISCONNECT statement is not issued, an implicit DISCONNECT and COMMIT are performed at PROC SQL termination.

The SQL procedure continues executing until you issue a QUIT statement, another SAS procedure, or a DATA step.

Arguments

You use one of the following arguments with the DISCONNECT statement:

dbms-name
> specifies the DBMS from which you want to terminate the connection. You can use one of the following values: DB2, ORACLE, RDB, or SQLDS, which refer to the SAS/ACCESS interface to DB2, ORACLE, Rdb/VMS, or SQL/DS. You must specify a DBMS name or use an alias (described below) in the DISCONNECT statement.
>
> **Note:** If you connected to the DBMS using the CONNECT statement, the DBMS name or alias you specify in the DISCONNECT statement must match the name or alias specified in the CONNECT statement.

alias
> specifies an alias defined in the CONNECT statement.

Example

The following example disconnects the user from SQL/DS and terminates the SQL procedure:

```
proc sql;
   connect to sqlds;
   ....
   disconnect from sqlds;
   quit;
```

EXECUTE Statement

sends SQL statements to a DBMS

Syntax

EXECUTE (*SQL-statement*) **BY** *dbms-name* | *alias*;

Description

The EXECUTE statement enables you to send DBMS-specific SQL statements to a DBMS supported by a SAS/ACCESS interface. You must have SAS/ACCESS software installed on your system to use this PROC SQL statement.

You use the EXECUTE statement to execute any SQL statement that is supported dynamically by the DBMS. In addition, the COMMIT or COMMIT WORK and ROLLBACK statements are also supported by the Pass-Through facility. Refer to the SQL documentation for your DBMS for details.

You can issue an EXECUTE statement directly without first connecting to the DBMS with some SAS/ACCESS interfaces (see "CONNECT Statement" earlier in this chapter). If you omit the CONNECT statement, an implicit connection is performed when the first EXECUTE statement is passed to the DBMS.

If your DBMS supports multiple connections, you can use an alias to direct the EXECUTE statements to a specific connection. To use an alias in the EXECUTE statement, you must first define the alias in the CONNECT statement.

Arguments

You can use the following arguments with the EXECUTE statement:

(*SQL-statement*)
    is any SQL statement that is supported dynamically by the DBMS, plus the COMMIT or COMMIT WORK and ROLLBACK statements. Any return code or message generated by the DBMS is available in the macro variables SQLXRC and SQLXMSG after the statement completes. The *SQL-statement* argument is required and must be enclosed in parentheses.

dbms-name
    identifies the DBMS to which you want to direct the DBMS statement. You can use one of the following values: DB2, ORACLE, RDB, or SQLDS, which refer to the SAS/ACCESS interface to DB2, ORACLE, Rdb/VMS, or SQL/DS. The *dbms-name* argument must be preceded by the keyword BY. You must specify a DBMS name or an alias for the DBMS (described below) in the EXECUTE statement.

alias
    specifies an optional alias defined in the CONNECT statement.

Useful Statements to Include in EXECUTE Statements

While the range of statements you can send to your DBMS is limited only by the SQL that the DBMS supports, some statements are common across the four database management systems. This section lists a few of the statements you can pass to the DBMS using the Pass-Through facility's EXECUTE statement. The

---

EXECUTE Statement *continued*

DBMS statements are listed in alphabetic order and include a brief description. For more information, see the SQL documentation for your DBMS.

COMMIT <WORK>	saves changes made to database tables since the initiation of the application program, the start of the interactive session, or the last COMMIT statement. Some database management systems do not support this statement.
CREATE INDEX	creates an index on one or more columns of a DBMS table.
CREATE TABLE	creates a DBMS table.
CREATE VIEW	creates a DBMS view based on one or more DBMS tables or other views.
DELETE	deletes rows from a DBMS table.
DROP	deletes a DBMS table, view, or index from the database, depending on how the statement is specified.
GRANT	gives users authority to access or modify objects in the database, such as tables or views.
INSERT	adds rows to a DBMS table.
ROLLBACK	reverses changes to database tables made since the initiation of the application program, the start of the interactive session, or the last call of the COMMIT statement. Some database management systems do not support this statement.
UPDATE	modifies the data in columns of a row in a DBMS table.

Example

The following example grants update rights to user GOMEZ on the Rdb/VMS table SPECIALPRODUCTS. Notice that an alias specified in the CONNECT statement is used in the BY clause.

```
proc sql;
    connect to rdb as textdb;
    execute (grant update on specialproducts to [qa,gomez]) by textdb;
```

CONNECTION TO Component

retrieves and uses DBMS data in a PROC SQL query or view

Syntax

CONNECTION TO *dbms-name* | *alias (dbms-query)*

Description

The CONNECTION TO component enables you to query a DBMS for data and to use those data in a PROC SQL query or view. PROC SQL treats the results of the query like a virtual table. In Release 6.07, the CONNECTION TO component can be used in the FROM clause of a SELECT statement.

You can issue a CONNECTION TO component in a SELECT statement directly without first connecting to the DBMS with some SAS/ACCESS interfaces (see "CONNECT Statement" earlier in this chapter). If you omit the CONNECT statement, an implicit connection is performed when the first SELECT statement containing a CONNECTION TO component is passed to the DBMS.

If your DBMS supports multiple connections, you can use an alias to direct the CONNECTION TO component to a specific connection. To use an alias in this component, you must first define the alias in the CONNECT statement.

Arguments

The following arguments are used in this component:

dbms-name
> identifies the DBMS to which you want to direct the DBMS statement. You can use one of the following values: DB2, ORACLE, RDB, or SQLDS, which refer to the SAS/ACCESS interface to DB2, ORACLE, Rdb/VMS, or SQL/DS. The *dbms-name* argument must be preceded by the keyword BY. You must specify a DBMS name or an alias for the DBMS (described below) in the CONNECTION TO component.

alias
> specifies an optional alias defined in the CONNECT statement.

(dbms-query)
> specifies the query you want to send to a DBMS. The query is prepared and described using the dynamic SQL features of the DBMS specified in the *dbms-name* argument. This means that you can use any SQL syntax the DBMS understands, even if that language is not valid for PROC SQL. You must specify a DBMS-query in the CONNECTION TO component.
>
> The DBMS query must be enclosed in parentheses and it cannot contain a semicolon because that represents the end of a statement to the SAS System. Also, character literals are limited to 200 characters.

Example

The following example retrieves a subset of rows from the NUMBERS table, which resides in DB2. Because the WHERE clause is specified in the DBMS query, DB2 processes the WHERE expression.

CONNECTION TO Component *continued*

```
proc sql;
select * from connection to db2 (select * from numbers where a>2);
```

Return Codes

As you use the PROC SQL statements and component available in the Pass-Through facility, any error conditions are written to the SAS log. The return codes and messages generated by the DBMS are available to you through the following two SAS macro variables:

SQLXRC   contains the return code generated by the DBMS.

SQLXMSG   contains the return code generated by the DBMS and descriptive information about the error.

See the examples in the next section to see how these macros are used.

Examples

This section contains examples that reflect the enhancements to PROC SQL in Release 6.07.

Example 1: Using the SQL Pass-Through Facility

The following example demonstrates how you can use the SQL Pass-Through facility to establish a connection with a DBMS supported by SAS/ACCESS software. It enables you to specify host-specific options, send SQL statements to that DBMS, and end the connection.

□ The CONNECT statement connects to the DBMS and enables you to specify host-specific options; in this case, it connects to DB2 and specifies a DB2A subsystem ID. You should check with your SAS Software Consultant to determine whether the arguments for your DBMS interface have been set to default values at your site.

□ The EXECUTE statements create a DBMS table, commit it to the DBMS, and insert rows into the table. The PUT macro enables you to check the SQLXMSG macro variable for error codes and information from the DBMS. For error information alone, change the macro to SQLXRC. It is advisable to check the SQLXRC or SQLXMSG macro variable after each statement or group of statements.

□ The CONNECTION TO component of the FROM clause enables you to retrieve data from the DBMS and, in this example, to display the data as output. Note that because the table resides in the DBMS, it cannot be specified directly in the PROC SQL SELECT statement's FROM clause.

□ Finally, the DISCONNECT statement enables you to disconnect from the DBMS and terminate the SQL procedure.

The following example illustrates the Pass-Through facility statements just described:

```
proc sql;
connect to db2 (ssid=db2a);
execute (create table language_skills
   (lastname char(10), firstname char(10), language char(15),
    native_lang char(3), yrs_of_exp numeric, fluency char(10))) by db2;
%put &sqlxmsg;
execute (commit work) by db2;

execute (insert into language_skills
   values('Jones','Fred','French','No',5,'fair')) by db2;
execute (insert into language_skills
   values('Gomez','Maria','Spanish','Yes',30,'excellent')) by db2;
execute (insert into language_skills
   values('Gold','Jerry','Hebrew','No',10,'very good')) by db2;
execute (insert into language_skills
   values('Schneyer','Samantha','French','No',8,'good')) by db2;
execute (insert into language_skills
   values('Conway','Miki','Japanese','Yes',40,'excellent')) by db2;
execute (insert into language_skills
   values('Schmitt','Eve','German','',12,'very good')) by db2;
execute (insert into language_skills
   values('Wong','Li','Mandarin','Yes',null,'excellent')) by db2;
execute (insert into language_skills
   values('Adeleke','George','Swahili','Yes',null,'excellent')) by db2;
%put &sqlxmsg;

execute (commit work) by db2;

title "DB2 LANGUAGE_SKILLS Table";
select *
   from connection to db2(select * from language_skills);

disconnect from db2;
quit;
```

Output 5.1 shows the results of the PROC SQL query.

Output 5.1
Using the SQL
Pass-Through
Facility Statements

```
                              DB2 LANGUAGE_SKILLS Table

  LASTNAME    FIRSTNAME    LANGUAGE        NATIVE_LANG  YRS_OF_EXP  FLUENCY
  ----------------------------------------------------------------------------
  Jones       Fred         French          No                    5  fair
  Gomez       Maria        Spanish         Yes                  30  excellent
  Gold        Jerry        Hebrew          No                   10  very good
  Schneyer    Samantha     French          No                    8  good
  Conway      Miki         Japanese        Yes                  40  excellent
  Schmitt     Eve          German                               12  very good
  Wong        Li           Mandarin        Yes                   .  excellent
  Adeleke     George       Swahili         Yes                   .  excellent
```

Example 2: Creating a PROC SQL View Based on DBMS Data

This example uses the Pass-Through facility and the SAS/ACCESS interface to SQL/DS to grant privileges from one database administrator (OLSLAVSKY) to another DBA (STEINBERG) using an EXECUTE statement. A PROC SQL view (SQLVIEWS.HOWFAST) is then created based on data retrieved from the SQL/DS ORDERS_1991 table using a CONNECTION TO component.

```
proc sql;
connect to sqlds(user=olslavsky password=ukraine);
execute (grant all on orders_1991 to steinberg) by sqlds;
%put &sqlxmsg;
create view sqlviews.howfast as
   select *, shipped-dateorde label="Days to Process"
      from connection to sqlds
         (select ordernum, shipto, takenby, processedby,
                 dateordered, shipped
            from orders_1991
            where dateordered is not null);
%put &sqlxmsg;

title "Data from SQLVIEWS.HOWFAST";
select * from sqlviews.howfast;
```

Output 5.2 shows the results of this PROC SQL view.

Output 5.2
Output from
SQLVIEWS.HOWFAST

```
                         Data from SQLVIEWS.HOWFAST

                                                                   Days to
   ORDERNUM  SHIPTO     TAKENBY  PROCESSEDBY  DATEORDERED  SHIPPED  Process
   ------------------------------------------------------------------------
      11269  19876078   212916              .  03OCT91          .        .
      11270  39045213   321783         237642  03OCT91    19OCT91       16
      11271  18543489   456910         456921  03OCT91    13OCT91       10
      11272  29834248   234967              .  03OCT91          .        .
      11273  19783482   119012         216382  04OCT91    14NOV91       41
      11274  15432147   212916              .  04OCT91          .        .
```

(continued)

Output 5.2
(continued)

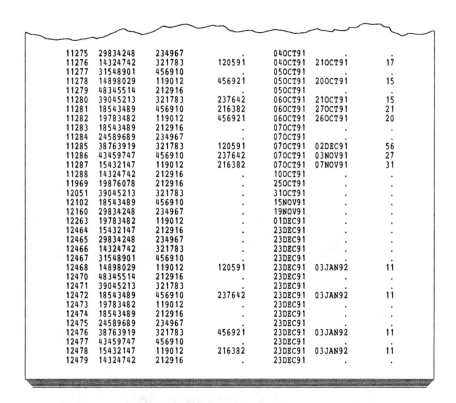

11275	29834248	234967	.	04OCT91	.	.
11276	14324742	321783	120591	04OCT91	21OCT91	17
11277	31548901	456910	.	05OCT91	.	.
11278	14898029	119012	456921	05OCT91	20OCT91	15
11279	48345514	212916	.	05OCT91	.	.
11280	39045213	321783	237642	06OCT91	21OCT91	15
11281	18543489	456910	216382	06OCT91	27OCT91	21
11282	19783482	119012	456921	06OCT91	26OCT91	20
11283	18543489	212916	.	07OCT91	.	.
11284	24589689	234967	.	07OCT91	.	.
11285	38763919	321783	120591	07OCT91	02DEC91	56
11286	43459747	456910	237642	07OCT91	03NOV91	27
11287	15432147	119012	216382	07OCT91	07NOV91	31
11288	14324742	212916	.	10OCT91	.	.
11969	19876078	212916	.	25OCT91	.	.
12051	39045213	321783	.	31OCT91	.	.
12102	18543489	456910	.	15NOV91	.	.
12160	29834248	234967	.	19NOV91	.	.
12263	19783482	119012	.	01DEC91	.	.
12464	15432147	212916	.	23DEC91	.	.
12465	29834248	234967	.	23DEC91	.	.
12466	14324742	321783	.	23DEC91	.	.
12467	31548901	456910	.	23DEC91	.	.
12468	14898029	119012	120591	23DEC91	03JAN92	11
12470	48345514	212916	.	23DEC91	.	.
12471	39045213	321783	.	23DEC91	.	.
12472	18543489	456910	237642	23DEC91	03JAN92	11
12473	19783482	119012	.	23DEC91	.	.
12474	18543489	212916	.	23DEC91	.	.
12475	24589689	234967	.	23DEC91	.	.
12476	38763919	321783	456921	23DEC91	03JAN92	11
12477	43459747	456910	.	23DEC91	.	.
12478	15432147	119012	216382	23DEC91	03JAN92	11
12479	14324742	212916	.	23DEC91	.	.

Example 3: Joining DBMS Data with SAS Data

This example uses the Pass-Through facility and the SAS/ACCESS interface to
ORACLE to show how data from a DBMS table (EXEMPT_EMPLOYEES) are
joined with data in a SAS data file, MYDATA.EMPLOYEE. It also shows how a
column-name list after the ORACEMP table alias is useful for renaming database
columns, for example when the column name is too long (FIRSTNAME); in the
column-list, you list all the columns in the SELECT clause, not just the renamed
columns. Using the NOLABEL option causes PROC SQL to display the renamed
columns instead of using the ORACLE column names.

```
options nolabel;

proc sql;
title "Joined ORACLE and SAS Data";

connect to oracle;
select fname,lname,sasemp.empid,gender,sasemp.salary format=dollar12.2
    from connection to oracle
        (select firstname,lastname,empid,sex,salary from exempt_employees)
                as oracemp(fname,lname,empid,gender,salary),
        mydata.employee as sasemp
    where oracemp.fname=sasemp.frstname
    order by sasemp.salary descending;
%put &sqlxmsg;
```

Output 5.3 shows the results of this PROC SQL query.

Output 5.3
Output from
Joining DBMS
Data with SAS
Data

```
                        Joined ORACLE and SAS Data

     FNAME           LNAME              EMPID  GENDER     SALARY
     ------------------------------------------------------------------
     VLADIMIR        MEDER              127845   M      $75,320.34
     MARGARET        MEDINA-SIDONIA     328140   F      $75,000.34
     CHRISTINE       DUNNETT            356134   F      $62,450.75
     LEONARD         DOS REMEDIOS       239185   M      $57,920.66
     CLARA           CHOULAI            129540   F      $56,123.34
     WILLIAM         LOVELL             457232   M      $55,000.66
     MARIE-LOUISE    WACHBERGER         212916   F      $52,345.58
     JUAN            RODRIGUES          459287   M      $50,000.00
     GUILLERMO       GONZALES           321783   M      $48,931.58
     STEPHANIE       HEMESLY            135673   F      $46,322.58
     SHALA           SHIEKELESLAM       346917   F      $46,000.33
     RICHARD         ARDIS              456910   M      $45,000.58
     R.              BATTERSBY          237642   M      $43,200.34
     G.              WOLF-PROVENZA       119012   F      $42,340.58
     CAROL           NISHIMATSU-LYNCH   677890   F      $37,610.00
     ITO             TAYLOR-HUNYADI     254896   M      $35,000.74
     PRUDENCE        PURINTON           216382   F      $34,004.65
     KARL-HEINZ      KRAUSE             456921   M      $33,210.04
     YUKIO           MIFUNE             423286   M      $32,870.66
     S.              HAMMERSTEIN        120591   F      $31,000.55
     GILBERT         SMITH              234967   M      $17,000.00
     PAUL            VARGAS             123456
```

Example 4: Retrieving Joined DBMS Data from the Same DBMS

This example uses the Pass-Through facility and the SAS/ACCESS interface to Rdb/VMS to show how three DBMS tables in an Rdb/VMS database are joined using an SQL SELECT statement in the CONNECTION TO component. Joining tables on the DBMS side is more efficient because you do not return all the rows from both tables to the SAS environment before processing the WHERE clause.

```
proc sql;
options linesize=132;
title "Joined Rdb/VMS Data Retrieved by PROC SQL";

connect to rdb(database='acct:[larsson]inventory');
select *
   from connection to rdb
      (select ordernum, stocknum, fibername, customer, name, dateordered
          from customers, orders, specialproducts
          where orders.stocknum=specialproducts.productid
              and customers.customer=orders.shipto);
%put &sqlxmsg;
```

Output 5.4 shows the results of this PROC SQL query.

Output 5.4   *Output from Joining Three DBMS Tables in the Same Database*

```
                       Joined Rdb/VMS Data Retrieved by PROC SQL

ORDERNUM  STOCKNUM  FIBERNAME    CUSTOMER  NAME                                                   DATEORDERED
-----------------------------------------------------------------------------------------------------------
   11285     1279   asbestos     38763919  INSTITUTO DE BIOLOGIA Y MEDICINA NUCLEAR                  07OCT91
   12476     1279   asbestos     38763919  INSTITUTO DE BIOLOGIA Y MEDICINA NUCLEAR                  23DEC91
   12471     1279   asbestos     39045213  LABORATORIO DE PESQUISAS VETERNINARIAS DESIDERIO FINAMOR  23DEC91
   11270     1279   asbestos     39045213  LABORATORIO DE PESQUISAS VETERNINARIAS DESIDERIO FINAMOR  03OCT91
   12051     1279   asbestos     39045213  LABORATORIO DE PESQUISAS VETERNINARIAS DESIDERIO FINAMOR  31OCT91
   11280     1279   asbestos     39045213  LABORATORIO DE PESQUISAS VETERNINARIAS DESIDERIO FINAMOR  06OCT91
   12466     1279   asbestos     14324742  SANTA CLARA VALLEY TECHNOLOGY SPECIALISTS                23DEC91
   11276     1279   asbestos     14324742  SANTA CLARA VALLEY TECHNOLOGY SPECIALISTS                04OCT91
   11278     2567   fiberglass   14898029  UNIVERSITY BIOMEDICAL MATERIALS                          05OCT91
   12468     2567   fiberglass   14898029  UNIVERSITY BIOMEDICAL MATERIALS                          23DEC91
   12478     2567   fiberglass   15432147  GREAT LAKES LABORATORY EQUIPMENT MANUFACTURERS           23DEC91
   11287     2567   fiberglass   15432147  GREAT LAKES LABORATORY EQUIPMENT MANUFACTURERS           07OCT91
   12473     2567   fiberglass   19783482  TWENTY-FIRST CENTURY MATERIALS                           23DEC91
   12263     2567   fiberglass   19783482  TWENTY-FIRST CENTURY MATERIALS                           01DEC91
   11273     2567   fiberglass   19783482  TWENTY-FIRST CENTURY MATERIALS                           04OCT91
   11282     2567   fiberglass   19783482  TWENTY-FIRST CENTURY MATERIALS                           06OCT91
   12475     3478   olefin       24589689  CENTAR ZA TECHNICKU I NAUCNU RESTAURIRANJE UMJETNINA      23DEC91
   11284     3478   olefin       24589689  CENTAR ZA TECHNICKU I NAUCNU RESTAURIRANJE UMJETNINA      07OCT91
   12160     3478   olefin       29834248  BRITISH MEDICAL RESEARCH AND SURGICAL SUPPLY             19NOV91
   12465     3478   olefin       29834248  BRITISH MEDICAL RESEARCH AND SURGICAL SUPPLY             23DEC91
   12272     3478   olefin       29834248  BRITISH MEDICAL RESEARCH AND SURGICAL SUPPLY             03OCT91
   11275     3478   olefin       29834248  BRITISH MEDICAL RESEARCH AND SURGICAL SUPPLY             04OCT91
   12464     4789   dacron       15432147  GREAT LAKES LABORATORY EQUIPMENT MANUFACTURERS           23DEC91
   11274     4789   dacron       15432147  GREAT LAKES LABORATORY EQUIPMENT MANUFACTURERS           04OCT91
   12102     8934   gold         18543489  LONE STAR STATE RESEARCH SUPPLIERS                       15NOV91
   11281     8934   gold         18543489  LONE STAR STATE RESEARCH SUPPLIERS                       06OCT91
   11271     8934   gold         18543489  LONE STAR STATE RESEARCH SUPPLIERS                       03OCT91
   12472     8934   gold         18543489  LONE STAR STATE RESEARCH SUPPLIERS                       23DEC91
   12467     8934   gold         31548901  NATIONAL COUNCIL FOR MATERIALS RESEARCH                  23DEC91
   11277     8934   gold         31548901  NATIONAL COUNCIL FOR MATERIALS RESEARCH                  05OCT91
   11286     8934   gold         43459747  RESEARCH OUTFITTERS                                      07OCT91
   12477     8934   gold         43459747  RESEARCH OUTFITTERS                                      23DEC91
   12470     9870   polyester    48345514  GULF SCIENTIFIC SUPPLIES                                 23DEC91
   11279     9870   polyester    48345514  GULF SCIENTIFIC SUPPLIES                                 05OCT91
   12288     9870   polyester    14324742  SANTA CLARA VALLEY TECHNOLOGY SPECIALISTS                10OCT91
   12479     9870   polyester    14324742  SANTA CLARA VALLEY TECHNOLOGY SPECIALISTS                23DEC91
   12474     9870   polyester    18543489  LONE STAR STATE RESEARCH SUPPLIERS                       23DEC91
   11283     9870   polyester    18543489  LONE STAR STATE RESEARCH SUPPLIERS                       07OCT91
   11969     9870   polyester    19876078  SAN JOAQUIN SCIENTIFIC AND INDUSTRIAL SUPPLY, INC.       25OCT91
   11269     9870   polyester    19876078  SAN JOAQUIN SCIENTIFIC AND INDUSTRIAL SUPPLY, INC.       03OCT91
```

There are still times when joining DBMS tables in the SAS environment is appropriate, for example, when the DBMS's SQL does not support outer joins. In the following query, PROC SQL performs a left outer join on Rdb/VMS data from two tables by using two CONNECTION TO components. Notice in outer joins that an ON clause is used instead of a WHERE clause.

```
select producti, fibernam, perunit, cost format=dollar16.2, ordernum,
       fabricch format=dollar16.2, dateorde label='Date Ordered'
  from connection to rdb
     (select productid, fibername, perunit, cost
        from specialproducts) as t1
  left join
  connection to rdb
     (select ordernum, stocknum, fabriccharges, dateordered
        from orders) as t2
  on t1.producti=t2.stocknum;
%put &sqlxmsg;
```

Output 5.5 shows the results of this PROC SQL query.

Output 5.5   *Using a PROC SQL Outer Join to Join DBMS Data*

```
                    Joined Rdb/VMS Data Retrieved by PROC SQL

                                                                      Date
        PRODUCTID  FIBERNAME   PERUNIT         COST  ORDERNUM   FABRICCHARGES  Ordered
        --------------------------------------------------------------------------------
             1279  asbestos    m         $1,289.64     11270   $2,256,870.00   03OCT91
             1279  asbestos    m         $1,289.64     11276   $1,934,460.00   04OCT91
             1279  asbestos    m         $1,289.64     11280   $2,256,870.00   06OCT91
             1279  asbestos    m         $1,289.64     12476   $2,256,870.00   23DEC91
             1279  asbestos    m         $1,289.64     12051   $2,256,870.00   31OCT91
             1279  asbestos    m         $1,289.64     11285   $2,256,870.00   07OCT91
             1279  asbestos    m         $1,289.64     12471   $2,256,870.00   23DEC91
             1279  asbestos    m         $1,289.64     12466   $1,934,460.00   23DEC91
             2356  nylon                         .         .               .
             2567  fiberglass  m           $560.33     12263     $252,148.50   01DEC91
             2567  fiberglass  m           $560.33     12468   $1,400,825.00   23DEC91
             2567  fiberglass  m           $560.33     11287     $252,148.50   07OCT91
             2567  fiberglass  m           $560.33     12478     $252,148.50   23DEC91
             2567  fiberglass  m           $560.33     12473     $252,148.50   23DEC91
             2567  fiberglass  m           $560.33     11278   $1,400,825.00   05OCT91
             2567  fiberglass  m           $560.33     11282     $252,148.50   06OCT91
             2567  fiberglass  m           $560.33     11273     $252,148.50   04OCT91
             3456  silk                          .         .               .
             3478  olefin      sq yd             .     11275               .   04OCT91
             3478  olefin      sq yd             .     11272               .   03OCT91
             3478  olefin      sq yd             .     11284               .   07OCT91
             3478  olefin      sq yd             .     12475               .   23DEC91
             3478  olefin      sq yd             .     12160               .   19NOV91
             3478  olefin      sq yd             .     12465               .   23DEC91
             4789  dacron                        .     12464               .   23DEC91
             4789  dacron                        .     11274               .   04OCT91
             8934  gold        cm       $100,580.33    11271   $11,063,836.00  03OCT91
             8934  gold        cm       $100,580.33    11281   $11,063,836.00  06OCT91
             8934  gold        cm       $100,580.33    11277   $10,058,033.00  05OCT91
             8934  gold        cm       $100,580.33    12472   $11,063,836.00  23DEC91
             8934  gold        cm       $100,580.33    12477   $11,063,836.00  23DEC91
             8934  gold        cm       $100,580.33    12467   $10,058,033.00  23DEC91
             8934  gold        cm       $100,580.33    12102   $11,063,836.00  15NOV91
             8934  gold        cm       $100,580.33    11286   $11,063,836.00  07OCT91
             9678  cotton                        .         .               .
             9870  polyester                     .     11288               .   10OCT91
             9870  polyester                     .     11969               .   25OCT91
             9870  polyester                     .     12470               .   23DEC91
             9870  polyester                     .     12479               .   23DEC91
             9870  polyester                     .     12474               .   23DEC91
             9870  polyester                     .     11279               .   05OCT91
             9870  polyester                     .     11283               .   07OCT91
             9870  polyester                     .     11269               .   03OCT91
```

Introduction

This chapter summarizes the upward compatibility changes to SAS/DB2 and SAS/SQL-DS software used in Version 5 of the SAS System. The chapter lists changes to the DB2EXT, DB2LOAD, and DB2UTIL procedures in SAS/DB2 software and changes to the SQLEXT, SQLLOAD, and SQLUTIL procedures in SAS/SQL-DS software.

Note: This chapter describes Version 5 procedures that run in batch mode under Release 6.07 of the SAS System.

All procedures in SAS/DB2 and SAS/SQL-DS software no longer support full-screen mode (that is, processing using windows in the SAS Display Manager System). For more information, see the *SAS/DB2 User's Guide, Version 5 Edition* and the *SAS/SQL-DS User's Guide, Version 5 Edition*.

Changes to Procedures in SAS/DB2 Software

Certain changes have been made to the Version 5 SAS/DB2 procedures so that they can be run in batch mode under Release 6.07 of the SAS System. These changes are described in the following sections.

Statement Added to SAS/DB2 Software

A new statement, the ELIMIT statement, is now supported by PROC DB2LOAD and PROC DB2UTIL in SAS/DB2 software. The ELIMIT statement specifies the number of DB2 errors permitted before each procedure terminates.

Statements No Longer Supported in SAS/DB2 Software

The following statements are no longer supported in PROC DB2EXT:

☐ the LIST statement

- □ the RESET statement
- □ the SAVESEL statement
- □ the TABLE= statement.

The following statements are no longer supported in PROC DB2LOAD:

- □ the DELETE statement
- □ the LIST statement
- □ the RESHOW statement.

The following statements are no longer supported in PROC DB2UTIL:

- □ the ADDCOL statement
- □ the DELCOL statement
- □ the DELETE statement
- □ the LIST statement.

Changes to Procedures in SAS/SQL-DS Software

Certain changes have been made to the Version 5 SAS/SQL-DS procedures so that they can be run in batch mode under Release 6.07 of the SAS System. These changes are described in the following sections.

Statement Added to SAS/SQL-DS Software

A new statement, the ELIMIT statement, is now supported by PROC SQLLOAD and PROC SQLUTIL in SAS/SQL-DS software. The ELIMIT statement specifies the number of SQL errors permitted before each procedure terminates.

Statements No Longer Supported in SAS/SQL-DS Software

The following statements are no longer supported in PROC SQLEXT:

- □ the LIST statement
- □ the RESET statement
- □ the SAVESEL statement
- □ the TABLE= statement.

The following statements are no longer supported in PROC SQLLOAD:

- □ the DELETE statement
- □ the LIST statement

□ the RESHOW statement.

The following statements are no longer supported in PROC SQLUTIL:

□ the ADDCOL statement

□ the DELCOL statement

□ the DELETE statement

□ the LIST statement.

Index